Busted with
Peter Robinson

First published in Great Britain in 2003 by
Virgin Books Ltd
Thames Wharf Studios
Rainville Road
London
W6 9HA

A catalogue record for this book is available from the
British Library.

ISBN 1 85227 004 7

Busted managed by Richard Rashman and Matt Fletcher
for Prestige Management.

Art direction by Paul West at Form® (www.form.uk.com)
Designed by Nick Hard at Form®.

Printed by The Bath Press.

Photographs:
Ellis Parrinder: 2–3, 7, 10, 12, 15, 16, 21, 22(L), 25, 27, 30, 32, 33,
35(L), 38–39, 46, 48, 50, 51(R), 52, 53, 56, 58, 64, 67, 71, 72,
73, 75, 77, 78–79.

James McMillan: 9, 11, 14, 19, 20, 22(R), 23, 26, 29, 31, 34, 35(R),
36–37, 41, 42, 43, 44, 45, 49, 51(L), 57, 59, 60, 61, 62, 63, 65,
66, 68, 69, 70, 75, 76.

Matt: 13.
James: 18.
Charlie: 28.

Contents

Hello, book buyers!

Well, would you believe it? You're holding our first book! The past year has been absolutely mental – from the release of our first ever single through the album and international success, all the way through to our massive UK tour. And it's all in here, with exclusive, never-before-seen pictures.

For the first time, you can read all about Miss Mackenzie, life inside the Busted house, how we really feel about girls, what we've got planned for the future and – if you're strong of stomach – there's a pretty unpleasant story about Charlie barfing in Matt's suitcase.

But while this is the true story of one year inside the Busted whirlwind, it's also the story of the years before we even met each other; those years when we were just three guys struggling with life's ups and downs with dreams of pop stardom keeping us going.

We hope you enjoy reading the book as much as we enjoyed writing it!
See you all soon,
Charlie, James and Mattie – July 2003

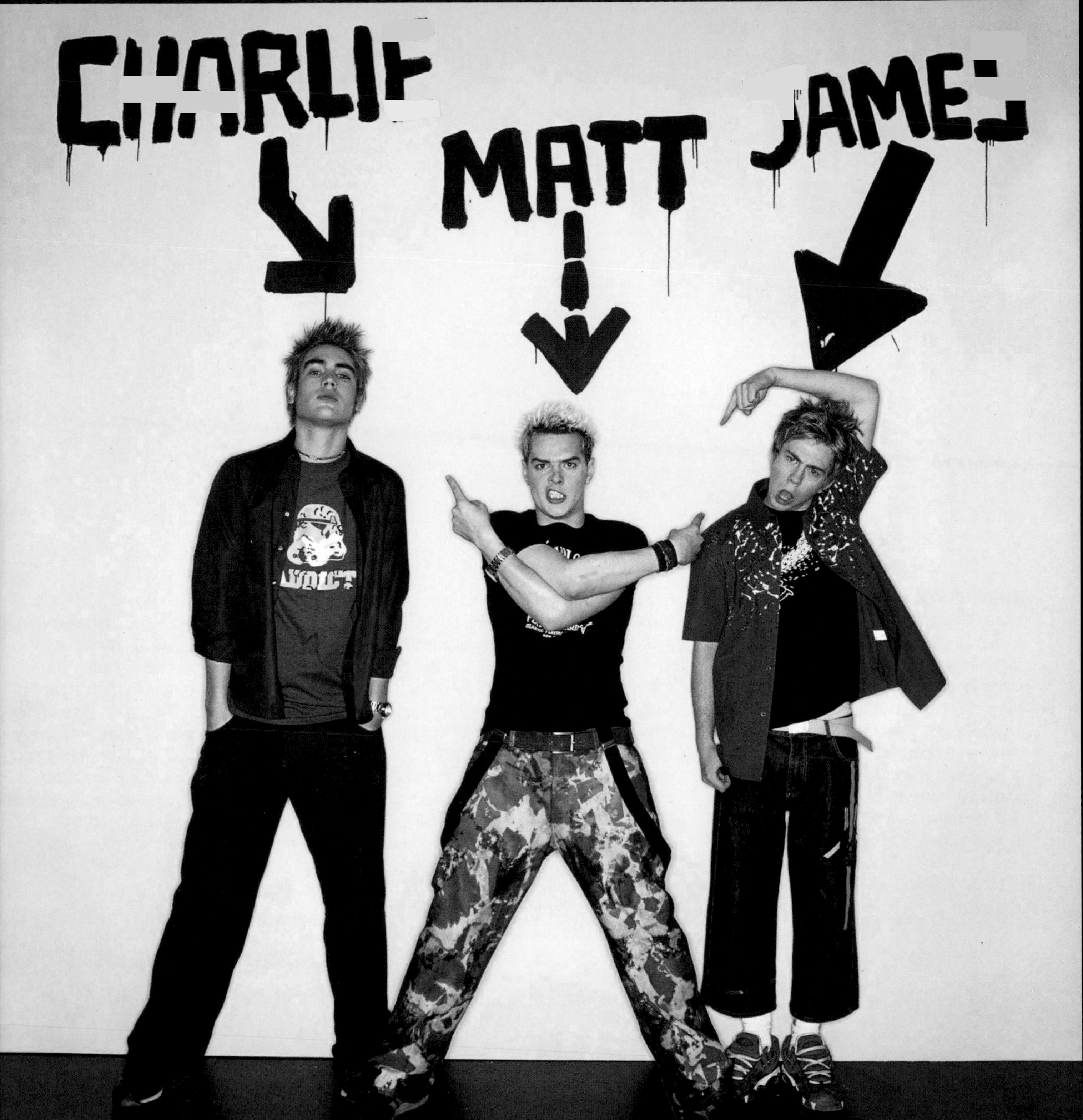
MATT

Mattie's Story

By the time I was 10, I'd broken 28 bones in my body. The doctors recognised that I was quite brittle-boned when I was a kid, but they could never pinpoint whether I actually had brittle bone disease. I think with hindsight I'd probably put it down more to the fact that I was being an idiot: I spent most of my early years jumping out of trees, climbing up walls and competing with myself to see how high I could get, or how near to the edge I could push myself. In some ways I haven't changed –

I still push myself to my limits.

My mum (Linda) and my dad (Kevin) met down a working men's club in the 1980s. At that point my mum was fourteen and my dad was nineteen, which was a bit scandalous in those days, and everyone told them that the relationship wouldn't last. In fact they were happy together for over a decade, during which time they had two kids. First was my older brother, Darren, who's now in a band called The Undecided. And then, two years later, I came along. I was born in Tooting, south London, but while I was still baby-sized we moved to Molesey, a suburban area of Surrey. Hampton Court is nearby and I remember that sometimes me and my mates would sneak into the Hampton Court maze at night and get totally lost. I don't think we ever figured that maze out. Some of Molesey is really posh, with massive houses all owned by millionaires. That's East Molesey, which is separated from the West, which is a really working class area, by a little alleyway. And right on that little alleyway is the house where I grew up.

My mum used to call me Fidget. I was never allowed E numbers in things like orange squash, because they'd send me mental – and I was always the kid who got lost when we went shopping, running off and getting up to mischief. I was quite independent as a child and I didn't like being told what to do. I was never indoors, either: there's a park just across from where I live where I'd be all the time. One of my earliest memories is of being round at my auntie and uncle's house. They're the biggest Elvis fans I've ever met. When we used to go round for Christmas and birthdays they'd always have his performances on the video, and they'd sit me down in front of the telly.

It was almost as if they were trying to teach me to be a pop star,

even at a really young age. Needless to say, I was captivated. He had this aura around him – he was cool, and legendary, and, regardless of what the music was like, he just was

Date of birth: 8 May 1983

Height: 5'11"

Weight: 11.5 stone

Eye colour: Hazel/Brown

Albums that changed my life...

1. The Streets
Original Pirate Material

Hearing Mike Skinner talking about his life is like he's talking about every Friday night of my life – coming out of a club, getting into a fight in a kebab shop … I was involved in that sort of thing but I never enjoyed it, and I don't think he did either. He's a poet.

2. Blink-182
Enema Of The State

The first album that really attracted me to the whole scene of being in a band for a living. I love songs like 'Adam's Song' – tunes that show Blink-182 are capable of more than cheeky chappy pop anthems.

3. Foo Fighters
The Colour And The Shape

I didn't even know this album was out when I saw it in the shop – when I got it home and 'Monkey Wrench' came on I just ran round and round my room for ages.

pop. He was everything a pop star should have been, I guess.

When I was three, my parents split up. It wasn't too difficult for me; after all, I was probably too young to understand what was going on. But I do remember my dad suddenly not being there in the house any more. It was weird, but I'd still see him almost every day, and he was always around when I needed him. When I got to school age, my dad would pick me up in the morning and take me to the sweet shop before school. It was something I'd always look forward to – he'd always have a joke for me in the morning, and I'd go into school and tell the joke and everyone would laugh. I remember that there was never much spare cash around. In fact, it was sometimes a bit of a struggle – my mum worked in pubs and my dad worked in a factory and neither of those jobs pay fantastically, but we were happy and it was a really loving environment. Around that time my mum met Brian, my

stepfather, and shortly afterwards they gave me my first sister. Amanda is fifteen now, and as I write this is preparing for her GCSEs. I hope she ends up doing better than I did!

At school I was mischievous rather than naughty – but I didn't find that I was inspired by lessons. It was something I did because I had to. My teachers were giving me hassle – once I was pigeonholed as being a troublemaker I'd often find myself blamed for things I hadn't even done. I literally couldn't do anything right, and it was a total pain in the arse. I'd get so frustrated. I'd come home and my mum would be on the phone to the school, and she'd go, 'Matt, what the hell have you been doing now?' Fortunately my mum believed my side of the story, and because my GCSEs were coming up she suggested that I moved schools to start anew. Bizarrely, the school I ended up at was the school my little sister was already at! I enjoyed that school a lot more and got involved

in the school plays, even though stuff like drama was desperately uncool for a Molesey boy. As it happened, though, I was only at that school for a year.

The change came one evening, when I was at a pub in Hastings with my family. It was a karaoke night and my mum made this big deal out of the fact that she'd never heard me sing, and made such a fuss that I agreed to go onstage. She wanted me to sing 'Love Is All Around' by Wet Wet Wet, but I thought, 'Bugger that', and went for 'Don't Look Back In Anger' by Oasis instead. I did my whole Noel Gallagher thing, finished the song and sat back down with my mum. Almost immediately I was accosted by some bloke who'd been in the audience, who explained that he was entering one of his own songs for something called the Vivian Ellis Award, which I later found out was an annual prize for songwriters. He explained that he needed someone to sing on his track

and that I'd be perfect. So I went over to his studio a week later. When I arrived I thought the studio was amazing, firstly because it had carpet actually on the walls, and secondly, more importantly, because I'd never been in a studio before! (When I look back now, I can see that the studio was actually a bit crappy.) I did the track for him and thought nothing of it – but a week later he phoned me up and said, 'I hope you don't mind, but I've heard that there's a scholarship going at the Sylvia Young theatre school, and I've put your name forward for it.' To be honest, I thought the idea of a stage school was a bit poncey, and nobody in my family had ever done anything like that before, so it was all strange territory. I said, 'Well, that's very nice of you, but I can't afford it', because I didn't understand anything about scholarships. But my mum insisted that I took the chance, so I went along to the audition, which involved a bit of acting and singing a song. I came out of the audition thinking I'd done OK,

but after a week had passed I thought I'd had my chance and blown it. Just when I was beginning to forget about going to Sylvia Young's, Sylvia actually phoned my house. She said that she loved what I'd done – but that the scholarship had already been given away. Then she offered me a deal – she said that if I went on her agency books for ads and TV programmes and things, I could pay off my fees using the money I earned. I'm still really indebted to Sylvia for taking me on.

I remember my first day at Sylvia's really clearly. My first reaction was, 'There are so many fit birds in my class. This is awesome.' There were about 24 girls in my class, and only 5 boys, which is the kind of ratio I like. But it was a total culture shock to go from my old school, where there'd be fights breaking out all over the place, to Sylvia's where the most dangerous thing in the corridors was someone pirouetting wildly by a window. I got a few acting jobs while

I was with Sylvia, but I wasn't too enthusiastic for three reasons. Firstly because

when I did things like The Bill and Casualty I'd always end up being cast as a drug dealer!

Secondly because I preferred the idea of immersing myself in a part, rather than just flicking into it and out of it for 30 seconds on the screen. And thirdly, most importantly, because by that point I was really getting into my music.

There had always been music around me when I was young. My dad, for example, had been a huge fan of Madness, a band I still love today – I think they've probably been a big influence on Busted, because they always wrote really well about what it

was like to be young, with a sense of humour and a real talent for pop songwriting. My brother, being a couple of years older than me, had got me into some of his favourite bands, too – bands like Green Day, and the whole pop punk movement that was coming over from America. When I was thirteen I entered a competition on TV to win a drum kit and somehow won it, so this huge top-of-the-range kit arrived through the front door one morning. Bad news for my parents but good news for me and my mates Peter and Chris – before long I'd formed a band with them and my brother. We called ourselves Sabotage. We were actually bloody awful, performed nothing but Green Day covers, and never played a single gig, but it was a really good laugh.

While I was still at Sylvia's I went into the recording studio for the second time, to help out a mate – Miles Slater – who was putting together a garage track. We recorded two songs – 'Sunshine Lover',

Icons

Dave Grohl

He started off as the drummer in Nirvana, and now he's just a total legend. He's such a great performer, too – without knowing it he's taught me a lot about what it means to be on stage, and how to be a performer.

Suggs

The lead singer in Madness – a really funny, warm, talented bloke. I'd love to sit down in the pub with him and let him tell me his stories; he's been in the music industry for years, but never seems jaded or bored by music.

My dad

Every single piece of advice, and everything he's ever said to me, has been right on the money. He's a clever guy.

which was rubbish, and 'Make You Mine', which I still really love. When that track went down really well in the clubs, I knew I wanted to pursue music. It was just a question of what style. I knew I didn't want to be in a rock band because I've always had a really commercial ear, but at the same time I hated all the pop music that was around at the time. But when I first heard Blink-182 I heard 'All The Small Things' on the radio, then saw the video a week later, and fell in love with them. I wanted to be in them. It really excited me, and it was just what I was after. Not long after that, I met James …

In a way I sometimes feel fake living this life now when my mates are still back home, working hard to do well for themselves. I've had to grow up fast,

It's just that I always knew I had something to do with me life.

I still think I've got something to prove, and something to do.

I'm not sure what that is yet, but I know I'm on the right path.

The Mattie I Know...

By his dad, Kevin

'I've started having to buy Smash Hits and Sneak to catch up with what Matt's up to! I get some funny looks in the newsagent but I'm proud to say that he's my son. I talk about him to my mates all the time – my head swells every time I mention him, and I'm always getting autographs for my mates, and their families, and all sorts. My fondest memories of Matt are when we used to go on holiday together and even then I remember him always loving being on stage, but he also loved coming out to play football with me, too. He had loads of energy and still does! His older brother's band are doing well too, now – I'm really proud of both of them. Maybe I'll be able to retire soon; I'm not getting any younger! Ha ha ha!'

James's Story

I've had a happy life – and a really lucky life, growing up in a loving, stable family with parents who wanted to see me excel in whichever career path I chose. But just before Busted happened, I experienced my first real-life dilemma.

Perhaps it was my independence that got me into trouble, but when I was seventeen it suddenly struck me that I had nothing. I'd ditched my girlfriend over a series of petty fights, I'd quit my college course in music technology and I was pinning everything on a band that would probably never even get off the ground. I had a terrible, sinking feeling that within months I'd be going back to college with my tail between my legs, begging to be allowed back in. All my eggs were in one really flimsy basket –

I felt like I'd totally lost control of my life

and one night, when my anxiety became too much to bear, I sat down with my

mum and we tried to find the answers to my problems. It had just gone ll p.m. and I asked my mum, 'Am I stupid to dream that this band is going to take off?' She looked at me, and grasped my hand, and answered, 'It'll happen, James. You'll make it happen.'

My determination is something I've definitely inherited from my dad, Peter. He's a self-made man, and built up a really successful import and export business from humble beginnings selling knock-off Ralph Lauren shirts to factory workers out of the back of his car. He'd approach any industry as long as he could see a business opportunity to be had – whether it was manufacturing diving equipment or selling the neon lights they've got beaming out over Piccadilly Circus in London. As his business grew, he'd often be away from home for weeks on end, but my mum, Maria, would keep me and my brothers and sister entertained back at home. She'd originally met my

dad through mutual friends when they were both fifteen and, when they decided to start a family, I was their first kid. Three more followed – Nick, who's eighteen months younger than me, then Melissa, who's thirteen and Chris, who's ten. You'll recognize Chris – he played our neighbour in the 'Year 3000' video and of all my siblings he's the one I'm most similar too.

We travelled a lot when I was young – my favourite ever holiday was to Disneyworld in Florida – but my first ever memories are of a strange house I lived in on Burgess Road in Southend. It was quite a small, terraced house which I've been able to describe in some detail to my parents in spite of the fact that we moved out of there when I was about ten months old – something they find a little freaky. My mum says that

when I was still in my pushchair I developed

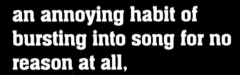

Albums that changed my life...

1. Blink 182
Enema Of The State

I can relate to the songs and to the songwriting itself. I actually love everything about that album.

2. Michael Jackson
Dangerous

It was a toss-up between this and Bad, but because Dangerous was the first time I went out and actually bought a brand new Jacko album it has to be this – it reminds me of how I felt when I first went to see him live.

3. 'NSYNC
No Strings Attached

This is where my Justin obsession started. The album was released in 2000, and it's got some of Max Martin's best work on it, too. The production sounds are really sophisticated as well – and 'I Thought She Knew' is a really great show-case for the band's voices.

an annoying habit of bursting into song for no reason at all,

and that there was no way of shutting me up! We moved again when I was eleven, to the house I spent the rest of my time in – it's a comfortable house and I was given the top floor to share with Nick. He's so different from me (we literally have nothing in common!) that we were the perfect floor-mates and we got on really well. We still do.

There wasn't actually much in the way of music in my house when I was growing up, so when I first got into music it was almost by accident. As a six-year-old I was totally obsessed with a skating place called Rollercity near my house. I didn't have in-line skates, just these dreadful, four-wheeled rollerboots, but I loved Rollercity and was down there every Wednesday night and Saturday morning. One day I noticed this

guy there in a T-shirt I really liked and he told me that the character on the front was someone called Bart Simpson. I've got quite an obsessive, inquisitive nature, so from the point when I noticed that T-shirt it wasn't long before I'd bought a record Bart Simpson made in the early '90s, called 'Do The Bartman'. One line in that song, about 'dancing like Michael Jackson' intrigued me, so I started trying to find out who this Michael Jackson person was. And when I did find out, I was amazed. My discovery of Michael Jackson is a key moment in my life. His albums, like Dangerous and Bad, became the soundtrack of my life and, as a result, the soundtrack of my family's life too.

The following year, when I was seven, I got to see Michael Jackson in concert for the first time. My friend Eliot bought me a ticket and it's still the best live show I've ever, ever seen. I'll never forget the feeling as we walked into Wembley Stadium that afternoon – it was as if I

could feel Michael's presence somehow. I knew he was near. Because we were still small Eliot and I took turns on his dad's shoulders to watch the show, but even when I couldn't see the show it was impossible not to get caught up in the excitement. A few weeks later at school (Alleyn Court in Southend – we had a horrible, pink-striped uniform), I was in a music lesson and we were all offered the chance to learn an instrument. I chose the guitar with one aim, and one aim only: to play Michael Jackson songs.

I'm the kind of person who throws himself into something obsessively and wants to be the best immediately.

I played tennis a lot when I was young and as soon as I started I wanted to be a pro from the word go – I wanted to be

able to do the fastest serves and the longest rallies. And in a way that was easier; after all, you can whack a ball across the net and let all your aggression out when it's not going well. But with the guitar it was hard work, and when I became frustrated and hammered away on the acoustic guitar all I'd get were bloody fingers. It was incredibly frustrating and from time to time I considered giving up, and it took a couple of years, but the first time I ever managed to play a Michael Jackson song – 'Earth Song' – on the guitar, I knew it was all worth it.

I always loved doing drama and stuff at school, and when I was ten a local theatre group put on a production of Oliver! The musical had really appealed to me because I loved the music, and I managed to bag a role as a member of Fagin's gang. Somehow (and looking back now it seems unbelievable), from that small first step, my next acting role was Oliver! again – but this time in the

West End of London, with the actor Jonathan Pryce. I'd been along to the open audition, which is the one all the kids who didn't go to stage school have to attend, and managed to get through, which was a real confidence boost for me as I'd had no formal training, either vocally or on the stage. I was part of that production for two years, though in short bursts because, still being quite young, the law said that I couldn't work for more than forty days at a time. Before long I'd progressed to the lead role of Oliver.

One really vivid memory of that time is appearing with the cast at the Royal Variety Performance in front of Prince Charles, but most of my friends were more excited by the fact that Robbie Williams' old band, Take That were back- stage. I had great fun chatting to teenage Take That fans by the stage door; Take That were at the height of their success, and I was at the height of my cheekiness, so I managed to convince all these sixteen-year-olds that

20

Date of birth: 13 September 1983

Height: 5'10"

Weight: 11 stone

Eye colour: Blue

I knew the band. Being only ten at the time, I was in heaven. The role in Oliver! led to a couple of dodgy acting jobs – I crashed a fire engine in London's Burning, for example – but it was never something I was too passionate about, because before long I decided that I wanted to make music for a living.

As I entered my teens, my musical tastes were beginning to develop. MJ still formed a huge part of my CD collection, but alongside Dangerous, Bad and the rest were CDs from bands like Green Day, as well as Robbie Williams, whose first album, Life Thru A Lens, had just come out. I really liked Robbie's humour and energy, and in some ways I can see that coming through in Busted today. As I was getting better on the acoustic guitar, my parents bought me an electric guitar as a present and from that point onwards I never looked back. By the time I was twelve I'd formed a band called Sic Puppy with my mate Nick. We were

really determined to make the band as good as possible, and some of the songs we wrote together still sound quite good, if not quite as polished as the material we've come up with in Busted.

Sic Puppy used to practice in either Nick's bedroom or mine. There wasn't enough room for our drummer, Jeremy, to get his drumkit in, so he used to have to make do on bongos, and for a long time we didn't even have a bassist, which was a ridiculous state of affairs but sounded all right to us at the time. Jeremy, Nick and I used to live quite close to each other, but dragging my guitar and amp round to Nick's house used to exhaust me. I remember sometimes I was so tired that I could only carry them ten paces at a time before having to put them down for a rest, and by the time I'd get to rehearsal I was knackered! We eventually found a new rehearsal space – in a warehouse – meaning there was room for a proper drumkit – and a bassist called Stewart.

Icons

Michael Jackson

Best dancer, best singer, best performer ever. He gets a hard time these days. I feel sorry for him.

Jim Carrey

He's the funniest guy. I piss myself literally every time I see him. He's quite a versatile actor, too.

Michael J Fox

The man's a legend. He starred in Back To The Future for a start, which is obviously my favourite film. I first saw it on a Wednesday evening on the BBC, then I got the video, then I watched all of the films. The third one wasn't as good as the second.

Two of my favourite songs from that period were 'Something's On My Mind' (which I now realise was heavily 'influenced' by Nirvana!) and a Green Day-esque number called 'Once In A While'.

The first gig we ever played was in the car park at the school fête! We'd stormed round to our headmaster's house mob-handed and demanded that he let us play there. Surprisingly, he agreed. We hardly had any material – in fact we just played the same three songs, over and over again – but it was brilliant. After that we'd play a few gigs around clubs and pubs in Southend but, especially in the early days, I was obviously under-age so I'd find myself kicked out straight after the gig. There was one where they wouldn't even let me back in to get my equipment!

Gradually, Sic Puppy fizzled out. It began when one week, instead of rehearsing on a Friday, we each decided to go out into town for a night out. Then the same happened the next week, and the week after, and gradually that old warehouse we'd use to rehearse in was used less and less.

One of my fondest memories of South-end is of a party I had at my house on Millennium Eve. That party still stands as the greatest ever – the house was being redecorated a few weeks later so I had permission to totally trash the place, and as a bit of a bonus every single girl there was really, really fit. It was like one of those unbelievable parties you see in films – and everyone was going, 'How on earth did you get so many fit birds at your party?' And I was just, like, 'I have no idea.' It was the best night ever – I'd go upstairs and there were, like, three girls sat on my bed! They were going, 'Oh, James, your party's just the best…' And there was one girl who'd been blown out who was sitting crying in my room – I was playing her tunes on my guitar. I was quite drunk by that point. It seems a bit cheesy now.

'Don't worry, lady – I have music!'

In 2000, I did my GCSEs and came out with pretty good results – two A's, one A, four Bs and three Cs, which wasn't too bad considering I'd done absolutely no revision! I decided to go to a local college for a course in music technology, and for the next year or so spent almost all my time cooped up in the college's recording studio, learning how to produce my own music. I was passing my assignments but I wasn't getting distinctions because, by this point, Busted was already beginning to take shape. In mid-2001 I quit my course without really having a definite plan of what I was going to do, because Busted was far from being a dead cert. It was a difficult time and I really felt like I'd messed my life up. As it happens, my life was about to turn a major corner…

The James I Know...

By music teacher Mr Puddick

'You can tell when a kid is good – and I knew that James would go on to big things. No challenge was too great for James; he put his heart and soul into everything. I've got a huge Busted display in my classroom at school and I'm getting my Year Nine class to write a pop song in the style of Busted. There are some really good ones coming out, too! In ten years from now I think James will still be in the music business – since school he's always been so creative and able to adapt that he'll always be around making music. I'm terribly proud of him.'

I wouldn't change a thing about my childhood. I had a really happy upbringing, with a close family and loads of aunts and uncles coming round to see me all the time. Some of my earliest memories are of playing in the garden of our first house on Catherine Street in Woodbridge – a small Anglo-Saxon town on the River Deben in Ipswich. Thinking about it now, there's not much social life going on there, but as a kid it was the perfect place to grow up.

Before I was born, my mother Tessa loved to travel – she spent a year in France, and six in America. It was in America that she first met my dad, Mike, who was over in the States on holiday. They got married in Britain, and started a family. My two older brothers appeared first – Will, who's now 23, and Ed, who's 21. I was born in Ipswich by caesarean section, probably because I was so huge even then! Mum used to call me Farley when I was young, because I was

addicted to Farley's baby rusks and it rhymed with Charlie, but if that makes me sound like sweetness and light you'll have to ask my mum about the time I decided I wanted to be a barber. She was asleep on the sofa at the time, so she never heard me getting the scissors from the kitchen drawer. Nor did she wake up when I set to work on her hair. By the time I was finished, there was more hair on the floor than there was on her head, and when I proudly woke her up and handed her a mirror so she could examine my handiwork, she let out a massive scream.

I was quite chubby as a kid,

with a little pot belly and a bit of puppy fat around my face, and my brothers used to take the mickey out of me about it. I got on well with Will and Ed until I was about seven, but at that point they were entering their teens and there seemed to be something of a gap

opening up between us. All brothers fight from time to time, but with us it seemed constant, and it really got me down for a while. Strangely, that lasted until I also entered my teens, so I suppose it's just something kids go through, and it seemed pretty bad at the time, but we're best friends now.

By the age of seven, I'd really got into music. My brothers had introduced me to their record collections and rock bands like Guns 'n' Roses and Metallica – I'd get all the posters from rock magazines and stick them all over my walls. I don't think my mum ever really approved of all that, but she and dad were happy enough to let me listen to the music. On my tenth birthday I was given something that would change my life forever: my first ever electric guitar. There's a brilliant photograph somewhere of me opening the present with this look of utter ecstasy across my face. I got to play that very same guitar in front of 20,000 fans at a gig last year,

which was a really special moment for me.

Just as music was opening up a whole new world for me, I was sent to boarding school in Norfolk and as soon as I arrived there I felt like my world was closing down again. The first night was awful – sleeping in a freezing dorm room with seven other boys I'd never met before. My parents told me to stick it out. And with hindsight they were probably right, but I began to resent it. Every night I'd be on the phone in tears, begging to be allowed home again. What made it worse was knowing that the school was actually only about half an hour's drive from my house – and I used to dream of crossing the fields which separated the school from the outside world and escaping. Eventually I was allowed to join my brother Ed at a school called Uppingham. It was also a boarding school, but having Ed around meant that I didn't feel as cut off, and I enjoyed it a lot more. It was around that

time that I began to make more friends back home, too. Because I'd been boarding, I'd lost touch with most of the people I'd grown up with, and when I'd be home for holidays I'd spend most of my time indoors watching the TV. But as my teens progressed I really made an effort to go out and meet people, which turned out for the best, because some of the people I met during that period are now my best friends.

When Ed went to senior school, he met a girl who converted him to Christianity. It was quite unexpected, and a pretty strange time in my family, because while my father had always been quite religious, regular church-going wasn't something that happened in the Simpson family. For a while I'd go to Christian meetings with Ed, too, and while I wouldn't describe myself as a regular church-goer any more, religion and spirituality is something that will always be quite important to me. It's just that as I grew older my lifestyle changed

and I began to feel that I knew my focus well enough on my own terms.

Mattie often takes the mickey out of me for being posh.

To an extent that's quite true – for as long as I can remember my family has been stable financially, and then when my dad became a partner in his chartered surveying company there was a bit more cash around. We've always had money when we've needed it, but I think a lot of people seem to look on my family as having it easy. Of course certain things are a lot easier when you don't have to worry about paying the rent – but there are still massive debts to pay, and unless you're a millionaire you still have to think about looking after the pennies. It's always put into perspective when I meet up with friends from school, some of whom are just stinking rich. One of my best friends' dads owns Umbro

Vital Statistics:

Date of birth: **7 June 1985**

Height: **6'2"**

Weight: **12 stone**

Eye colour: **Hazel**

Albums that changed my life...

**1. Jackson Browne
Live**

When I was much younger, my dad played it to me in the car all the time. The album's about him splitting up with his girlfriend and it showed me how to put real emotions into music.

**2. Silverchair
Frogstomp**

This came out in 1995 and it was a real inspiration to me. The band's singer, Daniel, was signed when he was just fourteen years old and I remember thinking, 'If he can do it, maybe I can too.' It took me three years longer than him though!

**3. The Deftones
Around The Fur**

One of my favourite bands of all time. I loved the fact that they could combine screaming vocals with really amazing melodies – it struck me as a totally genius concept and I still love it.

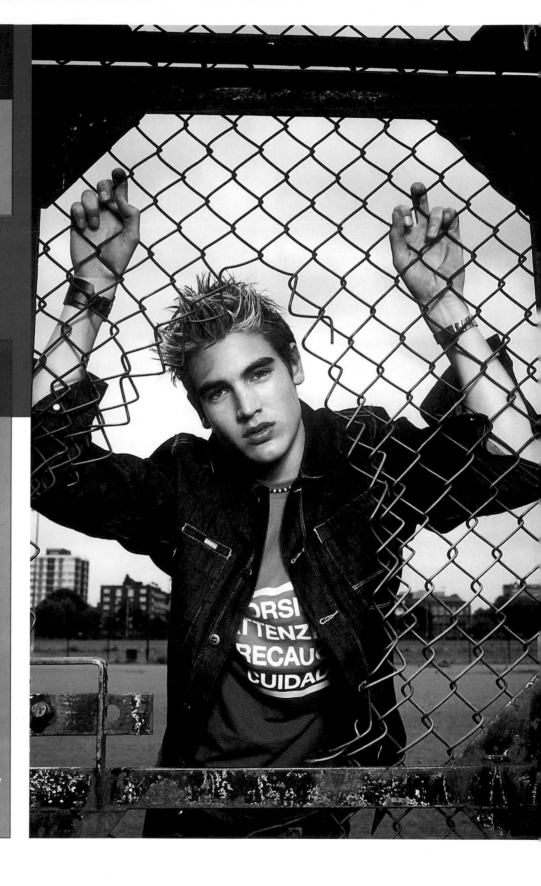

Charlie: Second from right

Charlie: Centre stage

Charlie: Centre

and is a multi-multimillionaire, for example.

From the outside it might seem like I've been spoiled and I'd hate for people to think that I've had it easy in life. Both my parents worked hard for what they've got now, and when they met, there wasn't actually that much spare money around. For this reason they've been quite careful to bring me up with my feet on the ground – I always got part-time jobs in the summer holidays and my allowance was only £60 a month until I left home, which was barely enough to keep me in drum skins! My parents' budgeting wasn't something I appreciated when I was a kid and demanding every toy under the sun, but it's a lesson I've learned to thank them for now I'm a bit older.

Having said that, I was so excited about Busted becoming a success that as soon as we received our first money from the band, all my parents' efforts went out of

the window and I went slightly mental. In the first year of Busted, for example, I went mad and blew loads of cash on things like drumkits, guitars, holidays and a car – as well as two lots of rent, because when I moved out of the Busted flat early in 2003, they insisted that I keep on paying up! Also, as I'm writing this, I've just had an offer accepted on a dark blue Porsche, which has always been my dream car. It's second-hand and I'm trading in my Mini to help pay for it. Hopefully when I eventually get to pick up the car I'll be luckier than with my Mini, which was rammed by another car within two weeks of my buying it! I'd actually only passed my driving test a few weeks earlier. I took what they call a 'crash course' (which always sounds a bit like it's tempting fate!) and passed the test on the first attempt, just six weeks after I'd first got behind the wheel. It'd always been my dream to be able to drive, and I sometimes think that my desire to travel and be independent was probably made stronger by those

years cooped up at boarding school.

I'm still not the most sensible of drivers, and all I can say in my defence is that I'm eighteen.

Back when having my own car was still a pipe dream, I was already in bands. The first was when I was about twelve years old. We were called Natural Disasters, which seemed like an immensely cool name for a band, even though it was actually suggested by my headmaster! It was myself and my friend Ian, as well as a few others, and our first gig was in a marquee for Speech Day at school. That was at the same time that a new music teacher started at school. My first music teacher had been into classical guitar and music that I found rather boring, but our new teacher had just finished working with Jamiroquai and was really cool, to the extent that

28

Icons

Kurt Cobain

He did so much for music and he had so much to talk about. What he did was just amazing at the time, taking rock music away from leather pants and curly hair. For one man to change rock music like Kurt did is just unbelievable.

Tom Hanks

He's such a versatile actor. When I was doing my acting at school he'd always be given to us as an example of the perfect actor. He's so totally gifted.

The Art Of Musicianship

That sounds a bit poncey, doesn't it? It's not something you can reach out and touch, it's just something in the air that someone can conjure up – the ability to change someone's mood through song. I think it's amazing.

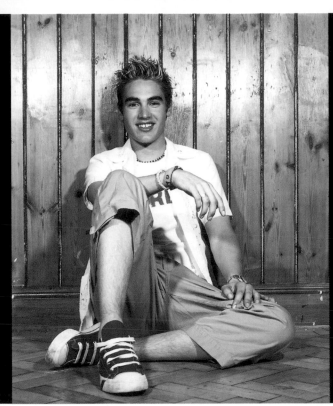

he'd actually tell me to pursue my dream of being in a band. I was in all sorts of bands during my time at school – another, when I was about thirteen, was me and my brother Ed's girlfriend and all her friends, so they were all about seventeen, and there was me, a chubby little thirteen-year-old on the drums looking absolutely ridiculous! Then there was Fubar, in which we'd play loads of Bloodhound Gang covers, and Manhole (where I really learned how to drum), and finally Spleen, with my mates Nick and Tom, which was great because it was the first band I'd been in where we didn't play any covers. Spleen took me right up to the point where I joined Busted.

Music has been with me through some really important moments in my life – some happy, some terribly sad. An example of the latter occurred in January 2003 when one of my best friends, Ed Brierly, went on holiday to Switzerland with his parents. They were staying in a

non-smoking hotel and he climbed up on to the roof for a cigarette. On his way down he fell five storeys and died when he hit the ground. It was a terrible time for all of us, and I was asked back to my school to sing Eric Clapton's 'Tears In Heaven' at his memorial service. The song had originally been written about Clapton's son, who fell to his own death in the '90s, so it's an emotional song anyway. All his family was there – and so were my family and all my friends, as well as people I'd never even met before. You could have heard a pin drop, and then the piano started. It was being played by the same music teacher who'd encouraged me to go for being in a band. Everyone was in tears, and I'll never know how I managed to hold it together, but I truly think it was the best I've ever sung in my life. I really hope I did justice to Ed's short life.

Like I say, music's the soundtrack of my life, and it's the most important thing in my life. Hopefully, some of the music I

make in my career will have a similar effect on other people's lives too.

The Charlie I Know...

By best mate Seb Rickard

'As a friend he's funny, warm and great to be around. I've known Charlie since he was thirteen – I remember my first impression of him was that he was a really sound guy, with a strange haircut. He had curtains at that point! He's such a laugh to go out with – he's the clumsiest person I know but at the same time he's really thoughtful. He worries too much, actually, he allows things to play on his mind. We've performed on stage together a few times and he's never hogged the limelight, even though he's clearly more talented than I am.'

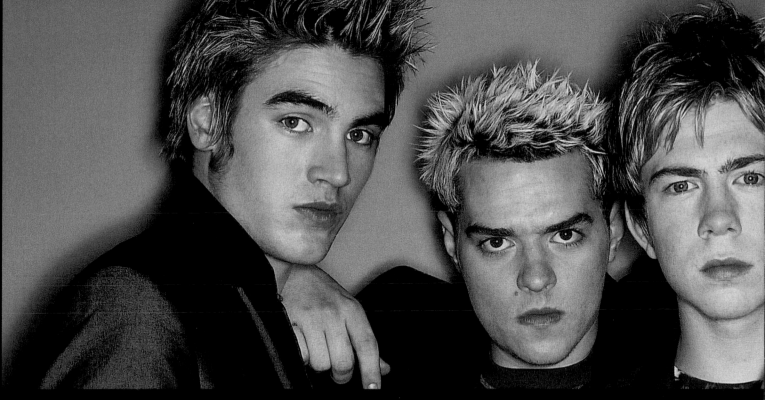

Making The Band

BUSTED

James: In 2001, I had become increasingly frustrated with pop music because, apart from some of the really good groups like 'NSYNC and Backstreet boys, there wasn't much that I liked. I'd met a guy in Southend called Fletch – he lived there and, as a musician himself, was someone who really helped me find my own feet as a songwriter. He was also a manager. He was partners with an American manager called Richard Rashman and one day he mentioned that he knew someone who'd be perfect for me to do some work with. I was up for giving it a go – so I spoke to this guy, Matt, and suggested he came round my house to try out some writing together.

Mattie: When I arrived outside James's house, this huge place looking out over the sea, my first impression was, 'This is bloody nice. I wouldn't mind a bit of this!' I knocked on the door – I can still remember hearing James's dog barking like some rabid maniac – and James

answered, rocking this pair of cream corduroy trousers, a Mambo T-shirt and this random cap perched on his head like some sort of surfer dude. We immediately recognised each other because we had previously met at gigs and acting auditions.

James was enthusiastic about writing songs right from the start.

James had just got £2,000 for some random acting job somewhere and had gone out and blown most of it on an eight-track recording studio and loads of equipment, which he'd set up next to the piano in his parents' dining room. He played me some of the tracks he'd been working on, and I was really impressed. One of them was a song called 'Living Without Your Love', which progressed to become 'Psycho Girl' on the Busted album. We sat down and began writing music together and it came really

naturally. The first song we wrote together was 'Sleeping With The Light', which was also on our album, but as soon as we came up with 'What I Go To School For' we knew that was the direction we should be going in – cheeky, stupid and funny with a killer chorus.

James: During this time I was still having a crisis. I was still at college, for a start. It was a really frustrating time because I knew Mattie and I really had a chance of making it work, but I also knew

the hard work had only just begun.

We didn't have a record deal, for a start, and from Sic Puppy and all my mates' bands I knew that it wasn't going to be easy. And all the time we had Fletch and Richard on the other end of the phone, like something out of Charlie's Angels, going, 'It's gonna be great, guys. Keep on with it.' My parents were pretty

dubious about the whole thing, and weren't too happy when I finally announced that I was quitting college for the band. It must have been difficult for them, but they backed me in my decision, even though I was probably as concerned as they were about where it would all lead.

Mattie: I was in a similar position. My parents didn't know what to make of the situation at all. Our manager Richard is an unusual guy – one of the most intelligent men I've met, and a great businessman. But his brain is so overwhelmed in business that sometimes he'd even forget to say goodbye on the phone. He'd just hang up. Sometimes I'd be on the phone to him, and there'll be a pause. Suddenly I'd realise two minutes had passed with nobody saying anything. Then he'd burst into action again – he'd just been thinking for all that time. On one occasion I went to meet him at the Intercontinental Hotel in London –

BUSTED

flash beyond belief, and the sort of place I'd never seen except in movies. When I arrived I had to go to the payphone in the foyer because I didn't even have a mobile at that point, and I called his room to tell him I was there.

I turned round and the concierge was there – and he tried to kick me out!

I told him I was waiting for someone and he went, 'I don't think you are, are you?' It was awful.

James: As the weeks ticked by, we knew we needed another member. We'd worked with a couple of guys in the early days and they hadn't really worked out, but we'd already booked ourselves into a studio and it was becoming more and more obvious that we needed a third band member. We took an ad out in the NME figuring that people who read that

would really be into their music, and booked an audition room at the Covent Garden Pineapple Studios in London. Even though we'd taken the NME ad, a lot of people still came along without any instruments or anything, but Fletch came up to us at the start and said,

'I've just seen this guy at the door. He's exactly what we need.'

Charlie: I'd been reading through the previous week's NME, just flicking through the gig guide to see who was playing that week. Then I chanced upon James and Mattie's ad, which was so small that it's a miracle I saw it at all. I'd been to a couple of auditions from ads before, but this one said that the band had management already, which I knew from past experience was a really important first step. I talked about it with my music teacher Mr French and he just went,

'You've got what it takes. Forget school and go for it.'

So I did. When I arrived at the audition I was given my number – 27 – and took my seat, ready to do my thing. The audition was right at the height of the first Pop Idol, so I think a lot of people who were there were just crazed on fame and being the next Will or Gareth.

Mattie: Charlie's audition was perfect, and I still think to this day that if he hadn't been at that audition, we wouldn't have accepted anybody else. When he told us afterwards that, as well as singing and playing guitar, he could also drum, we thought he'd been sent from heaven. In fact more accurately, at that point we thought he'd been sent from Holland.

It took him some time to convince us all that he

wasn't Dutch!

As soon as Charlie had done his audition, I wanted to just tell everyone else to clear off. It was so obvious to me that the audition was over. We knew we had the right guy.

Charlie: On 30 October 2001, James rang me at home. They were in the studio knocking some music out, and he was like, 'This stuff is sounding wicked! You should come down and hear it.' I asked why, and he went, 'Well, because you're in the band.' I couldn't wait until the next day to meet up with them, so we agreed to meet at their hotel later that night. Just after I got there, James ran down the road to buy a disposable camera, and we did our first ever photoshoot together. It was something of a shambles because we decided to do it in the toilet, reckoning that the lighting was better in there. Of course, we didn't have a clue about lighting or anything else and the photos ended up looking ridiculous.

James: The first thing Mattie said when we got the photos back from Snappy Snaps was,

'My God, that boy is tall.'

Afterwards Charlie admitted that he'd actually been intentionally crouching down in the photos because he was so paranoid about being kicked out for being too tall, but of course it didn't matter at all and in the end we made a point of Charlie's height – as anyone who's seen our album sleeve will know. The funny thing is that, that night in the hotel room, Mattie and I suddenly realised that we actually had to play some music for him, because he hadn't really heard any of our music. By this point we so desperately wanted him for the band that we were probably as nervous as he'd been at his audition.

Charlie: I'm sometimes a bit too cynical for my own good and I had been slightly concerned until that point that it was going to be pretty dodgy. The first song they played me was called 'What I Go To School For'. And I immediately thought, 'Great – this is not pop shit.' I'd grown up being in bands, and trying to be as serious about music as possible, and I was really relieved. It sounded real.

James: Christmas came along and all three of us went home to our respective houses. Loads of my mates were coming up to me and going, 'Come on then, you're a pop star, you reckon you're going to be famous, so when's your record out?' And it was difficult to know how to respond, because even at this point nothing was at all definite. It was really difficult explaining to them why things took so long. I kept in touch with Mattie and Charlie over the Christmas period and during January we arrived back in London, spent loads of time in the studio working on tracks, and started looking for a record deal.

Mattie: Bands can take years to get

signed. It's a long and depressing process of meetings, auditions, near misses and disappointments until you finally get signed – if you ever get signed at all. In January 2002 our managers set up meetings with some really big record labels and we played acoustic sets for each of them in turn. To be quite honest, I was absolutely shitting it. It was the kind of thing you see in films – and they use all the tricks in the book, like having your sofa lower than their desk, so they look important.

James: Some labels were more helpful than others. Sony was the strangest experience. I was wearing a Michael Jackson T-shirt underneath my shirt that day – and Sony are Michael Jackson's record label. Suddenly the A&R guy started going, 'Button that shirt up, Michael Jackson's an idiot.' He was slating Michael Jackson down to the ground – I just thought that if this is how that guy would talk about Michael Jackson, the man who'd made Sony what

it is today, then what would he say behind our backs? That guy never called us back, even to pass on signing the band, but by that point all the other labels were offering us deals, so it didn't matter! One of them was BMG, and

we'd played an acoustic set for Simon Cowell right at the peak of Pop Idol.

He was quite cold before he'd heard our stuff, and, as you can imagine, we were expecting the worst from him. Then after he'd heard us play, he waited for five seconds – which seemed like the longest time in the world – and said, 'Actually, I really like it'. He offered us £1 million to sign to his label.

Charlie: Then we went to Universal Island, and I'd always loved this band called dEUS who'd been signed to the label, so I was really into it already. We

went to see Paul Adam, the Managing Director, and his main A&R guy, Louis Bloom. The other two guys knew who Paul was because he'd been a judge on the first series of Popstars, but I didn't have a clue because I hadn't watched it. As soon as we met him we knew he was the right guy for us, a really nice guy. Universal didn't offer us as much money as BMG, but we were thinking about Busted in the long term, and it seemed Universal were, too.

James: It actually became quite a stressful time – there were labels pushing to take us out to dinner and fighting over who would get to sign Busted and we felt under a lot of pressure. At this point our managers sent us home for one week to relax and, when we all met up again, we agreed that Universal Island was the label to go with. We eventually signed to Universal Island on 5 March 2002. A few weeks after we signed, I bumped into Simon Cowell. He was in his black Ferrari and I went and

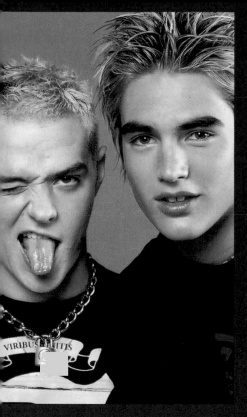

knocked on his window. He looked at me and just shrugged, as if to say, 'What happened?' I hope he understands, but at that point I don't think even we understood what was happening – or what was just around the corner…

What I saw in Busted…

Paul Adam, MD, Universal Island

'I remember when they came in the first time I'd just moved offices – I had a desk, a hi-fi and a telly, but no chairs, so we were all sat on the floor. They performed 'What I Go To School For', 'Year 3000' and 'Crash And Burn'. They were such bloody good songwriters and they absolutely blew me away – I wanted to lock the door so they wouldn't escape and go to any other record labels! I've worked with indie bands and pop bands and Busted immediately struck me as the next step forward – a combination of the two. And I got extremely excited about the boys, the songs, and the whole package. When they signed with Universal Island I was just over the moon!"

'What I Go To School For'

James: 'What I Go To School For' was written while Mattie was staying at my house in the summer of 2001. The way this song originally came about is the same way most of our best songs came about – by accident. We'll often start with an idea, or a concept, but this time it was just the line, 'Can't tell my mates 'cos they'll all laugh, I feel I'm heading down that path.' It suddenly popped into my head that 'member of staff' should be the next rhyme. Then I remembered what Mattie had told me that morning about his old science teacher, and from that point onwards the song wrote itself. Once we have a really good concept for a song, the rest tends to come really quickly.

Mattie: We got so excited once we'd finished. Before that we'd written quite a few songs, and a couple are on the album, but I knew at that point that 'What I Go To School For' was the first potential hit record we'd written together. It was the first one we could

really see ourselves performing on CD:UK. It was the song we'd been waiting for – and it really changed things. I suddenly thought, 'Bloody hell, we've really got a chance here.' It was one of the first songs we demoed in the studio, one of the first we played in our auditions for labels, and when Universal Island eventually came to deciding on Busted's debut single, it was the one we all chose.

James: With our first single in place, we started on our press campaign. The first step was to get some photographs taken to send out to magazines. So we had our first ever photoshoot for the label at the Trocadero in London, which is a huge shopping and games arcade. The pictures are really funny to look at now. We're in dodgem cars and I'm clutching the steering wheel and looking totally terrified.

It's shocking how inexperienced we were then …

...but it was great fun.

Mattie: I actually hated that first shoot, and it was only much later on that I grew to tolerate photo shoots. I had, and I still have, a problem with standing there being photographed. Charlie's fine – because he can pull off the moody look, and James smiles all the time anyway, but I always felt like a spare part, and I used to think people who did cheesy shoots were idiots. Perhaps I was right to an extent, but that's how my stupid faces started to happen. For the first shoot I was so uncomfortable that I just couldn't take it seriously, so started pulling faces which would eventually become something of a trademark. The famous Mattie Busted gurn, apparently. I still think looking 'sexy' for a camera is ridiculous, so

the idea of people having my face on their bedroom walls does my

head in.

Charlie: From the point when we signed to Universal Island, the label took the unusual step of having us play a gig, every Monday night, in the office canteen. Over the course of a few weeks everyone in the building must have seen us at least twice, and the acoustic sets turned out to be so popular that we took them on a tour of all the pop magazines, which was just surreal, meeting all the people who for the next few years would hopefully be interviewing us and reviewing our music. It was more nerve-wracking than the label auditions, but there was one magazine in particular that I was dreading visiting. When Busted were still waiting to be signed and money was running low, I'd signed on at the Models One modelling agency, and I'd been in to this one particular magazine with my book. They'd totally ignored me. The funny thing is that, when I arrived with the band, they absolutely loved us. I don't like to keep

track of people who've annoyed me as you end up getting really petty, but I was pleased that it went so well. On 27 May 2002, we started shooting the video. When we turned up on the first morning it was a really important turning point for us as a band – there were literally hundreds of people there, from cameramen and lighting people to extras and catering staff, and they were all there because us three had recorded one song. It was really bizarre, like we were making some sort of Hollywood blockbuster. The video took two and a half days to film. The strangest part of the whole thing was that ...

I had to run through a field in my underpants

as part of a dream sequence. In the script it had been James, but on the day he made up some ridiculous excuse about having hay fever, so there I was in y-fronts and a thong (to make sure nothing fell out) in a field. I wasn't too

amused at the time, but fortunately my friends saw the funny side.

Mattie: Compared with Charlie I got off quite lightly in that video – my star turn involved being bent over and spanked. I had to make it look as if I was enjoying it, which wasn't too hard. Once the video was finished, we played our first proper gig, which was at the ICA in London. The ICA is quite a posh art gallery, just down the road from Buckingham Palace. They usually have really sophisticated international artists having exhibitions there, so it was pretty funny that we managed to take over the whole place for the night. Loads of people from the media came down – all the magazines, all the TV shows and radio people, so we'd done the place up like a massive school hall, and there was bangers and mash for school dinners after the gig. All our families were at the gig and the first thing I saw when I stepped out on stage was James's little brother, right at the front of the stage, jumping up and down

and pointing at us. It was only at that point that we realised how hot the venue was. I was melting, and stood there on stage under the lights I felt as if I was going to die, but it was great to perform a proper gig at last – and I think it was a cross between our performance, and the free booze for the audience, but

everyone just went mental. It was wicked.

We did 'What I Go To School For', 'Britney', 'Year 3000', 'Crash And Burn' and 'Without You' acoustically, just as we'd done it when we were auditioning for labels and performing in the Universal canteen. There were loads of technical hitches with mics cutting out and stuff but we just blundered right on through. The funniest thing about the whole night was that two of my mates turned up and ended up trying to nicking a crate of beer, except they were caught by our managers and had to put it all back!

James: It was a great night. Between then and the single coming out, things moved so quickly. Smash Hits put us on the cover, which for a brand new act is really rare, and mocked up a classroom with dozens of Busteds all wearing different clothes, which must have taken them ages. I remember they invited us into the Smash Hits office to pick up framed enlargements of the cover, and when we went in it was the first time we'd been there since we'd performed for the writers earlier in the year. It really felt like we'd made it – even though it was still a while before the single was in the shops.

Mattie: It took some time for us to come to terms with how big Busted were becoming. When people were interviewing us about anything from our first crushes to what was in our fridge, it felt a bit intimidating. I couldn't understand what all the fuss was about – we were just three lads who'd made a record. After a while interviews became

a little easier, but it still feels a bit weird that people care about what colour our pants are!

James: The first time I felt any sort of fame was when I went home to Southend one weekend. There's a surf shop that I always used to go into called Exile. The bloke who runs it's a funny, eccentric guy – he's always there flicking through the music channels on the shop's TV. I went in a couple of weeks before the single was out and he decided he was going to try to find me on the telly. Almost immediately he found the Busted video, and just stood there, pointing at me, then pointing at the telly, then pointing back at me. And then he went, 'There you are! How queer!' My mates and I just fell about laughing.

Charlie: When the single did eventually come out on 16 September, it was something of a shambles. For some reason loads of the record shops in

London weren't actually selling our single on the first morning – but by the end of the day it was all sorted out. Looking back now I think we can all laugh about that but at the time we were storming around in a right old strop thinking that we'd end up being robbed of the number one spot. Seeing 'What I Go To School For' on the shelves at our local Virgin Megastore was a huge deal, though – we all went down on the Monday and bought a copy each. (Actually, we bought three each, but let's keep that quiet.) It was funny to see our record on the shelf. It just looked so stupid among all these huge, international chart acts.

Mattie: On the Tuesday we found out that, from the sales so far,

the single was going to be a massive hit

which was a relief! When I got the phone call I was at my mum's house.

She was out shopping and I was having a lie-in. I was woken up by the phone ringing and it was Fletch, telling me that the single was heading for number three! I didn't know what to do! There was nobody to jump up and down with. So I made myself a cup of tea and sat down to consider it. It was just amazing. James: By the Sunday, when the official charts were being announced, we were already on our way to Germany, for our first international promotional trip. We were at the airport when Mattie called Dr Fox from his mobile for a live chat on the chart countdown. Charlie and I were stood there checking in our luggage, and Mattie was being broadcast live to the country as our single went in at number three. That was a crazy evening – we got to Germany and immediately went out on the town to celebrate.

Mattie: The following week, we performed the single on Top Of The Pops. It was the first time we'd been on the show and it was the most nervous

There's something about Busted...

Lisa Smosarski
Editor, Smash Hits

'We were so excited at Smash Hits when we first met Busted. The thing we loved most about them was the fact that they were a complete breath of fresh air. For such a long time we had seen reality TV acts dominate the charts – Busted were a band who were in it for their love of music. Busted were the answer to our prayers. We knew Busted were going to be huge and as soon as we saw the video for "What I Go To School For" we knew we had to have them on our cover. The boys were brilliant on the shoot and the cover looked excellent. We shot them in a school – it was one of our best shoots ever. From that day on we haven't looked back. The Busted boys are doing brilliantly – but we always knew they would.'

I've ever felt about anything, especially because David Bowie was in the studio too, and he's a total legend as far as I'm concerned. When I get nervous I pace up and down, and I was doing some serious pacing that day, but I saw some fans we knew and they talked me out of my nerves. But I still knew it had to be excellent. I remember coming off stage after the performance and we all thought it had gone really well – then we watched it on TV the following day and we all just held our heads in our hands. There were off notes all over the place, we couldn't figure out where any of them were coming from – it was just a shambles. It was a mess! So we knew that from that point onwards that we had to rehearse it a little more. And there would be more songs to rehearse too – because by that point our album release was just around the corner...

Blimey! It's the real Miss Mackenzie!

'At school Mattie was exactly the same as he is in his videos – he'd get his work done, but he was always having a laugh, and he was cheeky, chatty and charming. I couldn't believe it when I found out he'd written a song about me. In fact I refused to believe it until Mattie actually told me himself. It was five years ago [that I taught him] and he was actually a bit embarrassed when he told me last year – probably the first time I've seen him embarrassed. It's very flattering and some of my students now are aware of it, but I'd like to point out right now that none of the events in the song actually happened! Unless he actually did hide outside my house ... But I'm pretty sure he didn't! Actually I think we're going to meet up soon, so hopefully it will be okay! Any funny business? Certainly not!'

The Album

BUSTED

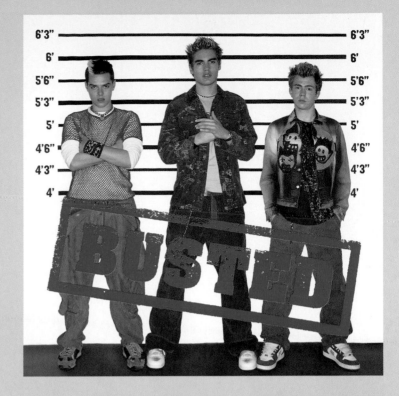

Charlie: Our debut album, Busted, was released just two weeks after 'What I Go To School For'. Because it was released so soon after the single, we'd actually been recording it while we were promoting the single, but the story starts a long time before that – before we even had a record deal. It's really interesting now to listen to those early eight-track demos Mattie and James recorded back in Southend – 'Psycho Girl' and 'Year 3000' all sound really different, and 'What I Go To School For' in particular sounds like a ballad! The reason for this, James has since admitted, is that on his original eight-track recording the drums accidentally recorded at half speed, so he had to record the rest of the track around that! With that in mind, we needed some top producers for the album, so we approached Steve Robson and John McLaughlin – who between them have worked with everyone from Def Leppard to Atomic Kitten, so we knew they'd be able to appreciate all the different angles we were coming from as

songwriters. They really helped to make our songs sound like proper hit singles – which is something of a miracle given the state of the studios we were recording in!

Mattie: We recorded the album at Brick Lane Studios in London. When I heard we'd be recording there I was well chuffed because I'd often go down Brick Lane with my mates to some of the clubs in the area, or for curries, as the place is full of Indian restaurants. Sometimes James, Charlie and I would end up going for a massive meal after recording, but more often than not we'd be stuck in the studio until long after the restaurants had all closed, with John and Steve refusing to let us out of the building until we'd been through every song dozens of times. To make matters worse the studio was, shall we say, a little run down – or, to be more precise, an absolute dump! It was a tiny little room with a curtained-off section at one end, which was the vocal booth. And there was a hole in the

ceiling, with water dripping in on us when we were trying to sing! Which seems quite funny now, but at the time really did my head in.

James: Writing the album had been a really steep learning curve for me. I used to write songs when I was in Sic Puppy, but they're nothing like I write now, and I think I'm a much more a polished writer than I was, say, five years ago. Most of it's down to meeting Charlie and Mattie – having two other brains working with you throws up so many different ideas and possibilities. It's weird, really, because Charlie and I come from such different musical backgrounds. I love the sophisticated pop songwriting of people like Max Martin, who wrote all the huge Britney and 'NSYNC songs, and Charlie's into sensitive indie and rock. From my perspective, songs are there to be popular – and from Charlie's, songs are there to make a statement. Charlie and I always disagree on this but I do

maintain that it's more of a challenge to write a pop song than an indie song.

Charlie: I'd never written pop songs before, and when I was growing up I was writing songs for myself, so if someone had asked me to change something, I would have told them to bugger off. I had a few arguments with James and Mattie about it – I was stuck in the old indie ethic about 'We make our music and, if anyone else likes it, that's a bonus.' What writing and recording the album taught me is that it's possible to make music which satisfies my creative heart, but which will also appeal to a mass audience. Songs like 'Without You' are really good examples of that, I think. And if I want to be a bit self-indulgent every now and again, I just keep the songs to myself.

James: There were times we'd argue with the producers, too, when they'd make suggestions on how to change the songs. It's like if you paint a picture in your art class and a science teacher comes up and goes, 'The sky is the wrong colour', you'll want to slap them. Something that I also had in the back of my mind – probably more than Charlie, actually – was the fact that if the album came out and the producers' names were added to the writing credits, people would assume that Busted were like any other pop band out there, and that we hadn't written many of the songs at all. And that's what happened – even now, people who want to get at us will say, 'Look at the album credits – they didn't even write their own songs', just because Steve and John's names have been added. But like I say, it's all part of the learning curve, and what Steve and John did with the album was amazing.

Charlie: The only time I really lost it was when my song, 'Without You', had Steve's name added to it. I wrote that song four years ago, at school. All my mates know it. So now it's there on the album with someone else's name added

– but if anyone comes up to me and says, 'You didn't write that song', I'll punch them in the face.

We're still asked ten times a day, 'Do you write your own stuff?'

It's so hard to explain to people that, when producers add a riff here or a production effect there, they end up becoming co-writers of a song, even if the tune and the lyrics are something Mattie, Charlie and myself have come up with. But that's just something we had to learn about the music industry, and the job Steve and John did with the album – including some of the bits they added to songs – was astounding. It was just what we were after.

Mattie: I was so happy with the album – and when it started getting good reviews from people like NME, The Times and Q as well as the pop mags, I thought we'd

really broken through. Unfortunately, when Busted actually hit the shops, the story wasn't quite so good. In fact it was ridiculous – the album flopped into the charts at 30, and then three weeks later it was down into the hundreds. At one point it was at number 141. I couldn't believe it.

Charlie: When the album got off to a slow start, I got seriously worried about what the label would think. Pop bands have always been judged on their immediate record sales, but the current climate in the music industry means that even indie bands have to prove themselves immediately, or they get the chop. Fortunately our label and managers kept telling us that everything was fine – that it was unusual to bring out our first album right after the first single and that it would eventually explode. We knew that our second single had to be a hit for us to stand a chance. The funny thing is that when we were first discussing the follow-up to 'What I

Go To School For' and

everyone started going mad for 'Year 3000',

I started to drag my heels slightly because I'd never been too sure about it as a single and wanted to release something a bit more serious like 'Without You'. As it turned out, 'Year 3000' turned out to be the song that probably really launched Busted. As soon as the song started getting played on the radio, the album sales started to pick up – and by the time 'Year 3000' was about to be released, the album had zoomed up to the top ten. I'm sure that when the album started going back up the charts, the label was as relieved as we were.

James: I loved the idea of 'Year 3000' as a single, mainly because I was really excited about seeing the song brought to life in the video. Mattie and I had written the song literally two feet away from

where we'd first come up with 'What I Go To School For'. We'd just been messing around with lyrics – singing a line, then singing another line, and somehow we got on to time travel. Some songwriters I really admire will be writing songs to a really strict brief from their record labels, or their management, but we were just trying everything out. All of our really good songs have come really quickly – almost out of nowhere. When it came to the video, I loved the treatment the director wrote for us, though I have to admit that most of the shoot was quite boring because the cartoons were added in afterwards. We all loved shooting the performance footage, though. It was shot at a live music venue called The Garage, in north London, which we hired out for the day. It took a while to get it right – and

Mattie had to shoot his crowd-surfing part twelve times because

fans in the crowd kept grabbing his bits and making him laugh!

After we show the video, we performed on the Smash Hits Poll Winners' Party, which was an amazing experience for all of us. We'd been watching the show every year for as long as any of us could remember, and to be finally on the show was surreal.

Mattie: When 'Year 3000' came out it was a difficult week to release a single, but the label said, 'It'll be top three.' As with the first single, we each went down to our local Virgin Megastore on the Monday and bought a few copies each, though we'd forgotten that we were a bit more famous this time round and we probably looked pretty desperate buying our own record! While I was in the shop, there was one girl there with her mum. The mother was attempting to persuade her daughter to buy the Kelly Osbourne single, but the kid was having

absolutely none of it. 'I like Busted,' she said. Repeatedly. It's funny to see that sort of thing happening, knowing what's going through people's minds when they buy our music. James's brother works in Waitrose and says that

kids sometimes refuse to leave the shop until their parents buy them a copy of the Busted album,

which sounds hilarious. It freaks me out now that people listen to my album on their Walkman or in their car — there's half a million of those people out there just in the UK, and probably more when you think about people robbing us of valuable beer money by copying it for their mates. It really does my head in when I begin to think about it. People have gone out of their house with fifteen quid, and gone into a shop, and actually

bought our album – instead of something else. It's just bizarre.

James: When we performed 'Year 3000' for the first time on The Saturday Show, Uri Geller was there too, and he took the opportunity to take us under his wing and give us a lecture us on the trappings of pop fame. First of all he bent us a spoon, then he took us into his dressing room, sat us down, and gave us the benefit of his advice. This is the guy who's known all the greats, like Elvis and Michael Jackson, all the way through to Justin Timberlake, so we guessed he'd know what he was alking about.

Mattie: Uri's advice was basically, 'Have a brilliant time, make the very most of everything, but don't get into drugs.' 'You know,' he said, 'I've seen it so much. You get into the industry and it's paved with drugs. Stay your own man.' The funny thing is that since I've got into the music business, I don't think I've been

offered drugs once, unless it was so subtle that I didn't even notice it. I think that even if I wanted to find drugs I'd have difficulty – though you look at what some people are wearing on CD:UK and you know it's a fair bet that their stylists are probably on some pretty strong narcotics.

James: When 'Year 3000' went in at number two, we just couldn't believe it. And the way it hung around in the charts shocked us all. We were presented with a gold disc for the album live on stage at Top Of The Pops Saturday, which was a total surprise because, even though we knew the album had gone gold, we'd forgotten that we got a disc to go with it! The album sold its 100,000th copy on 20 January 2003 and we went out and had a huge celebration dinner – then 'Year 3000' actually ended up being in the charts for even longer than 'What I Got To School For'.

It was in the top 30

for over three months,

in the end – and at the end of play was in the charts for longer than acts who'd been at number one while we were in the top five. As our profile grew in the media, we also noticed that the rumours about ourselves were getting more and more strange. There were stories that we'd each been given Porsches by our record label, that I was going out with Avril Lavigne – even that we'd each got our manhoods pierced! (There was also a rumour that Charlie had had a date with Britney Spears, though he later admitted that he'd made that one up himself.) Fortunately we've always had quite a good relationship with the press, and beyond a few silly stories like that I don't really think we've done anything to warrant a full-on tabloid scandal … yet!

Mattie: When it came to releasing a third single from the album, we found that we were spoiled for choice, but we wanted

to move away slightly from the 'high concept' songs like 'What I Go To School For' and 'Year 3000' – so we chose 'Crash And Burn', which was a bit less jokey but still had Busted's personality running through it.It was another song that we'd written quite early on I remember we'd actually arranged to sit down for a writing session, which was quite an unusual step, and Charlie was talking about how he'd been blown out.

He used the expression 'I crashed and burned', which isn't something I'd ever heard before.

Then we tied that in with a song we already had, which was a girl who literally was so fit, and she knew it. I love the way it starts – really gritty, for a pop record – and the song still sounded fresh even though the album had been out for a while, so it was perfect. In

March we'd just announced our first ever Busted tour, so we wanted the video to reflect the energy we were going to be putting into our live shows and with all the stunts at the skate park it turned out to be my favourite video so far. In fact, before filming started the director actually told me not to gurn in the video, but I was so comfortable with the video itself that I didn't feel it necessary to pull any stupid faces anyway. The hilarious thing is that all our names flash up on the screen, and but they finished the video they somehow got James's name wrong and it went out to all the TV shows introducing someone called 'James Harris'! It had been all the way through all the levels at Universal Island and nobody had noticed! Hilarious!

James: We knew it was going to be tough to follow the success of 'What I Go To School For' and 'Year 3000', because by this point half a million people had bought the album, so they already had 'Crash And Burn' in their CD collections.

So because of this, and because the album had been out for about half a year by this point we decided to give the song a bit of a spring clean and we each recorded our own personal versions of the track, with one on each CD (and one on the cassette, too). We also recorded a cover of the old Simon and Garfunkel track 'Mrs Robinson' for a b-side, which ended up becoming a bit of an acoustic favourite with fans and helped give us – to everyone's surprise – our first ever number one single!

Charlie: We couldn't believe it when we heard the news that Sunday – and then someone at the record label told us that we'd made chart history as the first and only act whose first three singles got to number three, then two, then one!

Mattie: When we went on CD:UK and Top Of The Pops I decided to wear some celebratory eyeliner, and we also had Charlie playing drums. We went on CD:UK with a load of kids of BMXs doing

stunts on a halfpipe behind us, as we all agreed that it was a great to get Charlie playing drums in the video. I love the way Charlie looks when he drums – it's so great seeing him behind that kit, just over the moon and banging away in his own little world. It was great practice for the tour, too, because by the time the single was in the charts, we'd already begun rehearsing for our tour...

Busted – What the papers said...

'There's much more to Busted than loud one-liners.' Sneak

'The best album about being a teenager in recent memory.' NME

'Busted are set to kick some boyband butt... A rock-inspired masterpiece.' Smash Hits

'Proof that Busted will be no one-hit wonders.' Sugar

'Melodic hooks by the score with attitude, teen angst and humour... A winning formula.' Music Week

'All hail the new punk-pop explosion!' Top Of The Pops magazine

'These boys've got talent – and they look good, too!' Mizz

'Packed with catchy punk-pop tunes with a sense of humour.' The Times

'Inspired one-liners and clever gimmicks ... The concept is a winner.' Q

'Year 3000' – What the papers said...

'If you're not already obsessed with Busted, this rawktastic track will change all that.' J-17

'After a few listens you'll be hooked – grab that air guitar!' TV Hits

'Their next hit – full of jerky, hacksaw guitars and ferociously catchy choruses.' Heat

'These boys have a bloody catchy tune on their hands!' Boyz

'Music as it should be – exciting, tuneful and able to hold your interest for more than a week.' Smash Hits

'A song good enough to grace the top of the chart at any time of the year.' Sneak

'Fun, full of cheeky, knowing humour and extremely catchy melodies.' Hello!

'Never mind "Year 3000", it looks like Busted's year could well be 2003.' Music Week

Busted In The House

Mattie: We moved into a flat in north London two weeks before we signed a record deal, but before that I'd already been living with James for some time, at his parents' house in Southend. The first few times I stayed there, I'd crashed on James's floor, but before long his mum and dad had borrowed a bed from James's gran's house and turned their spare room into a bedroom, just for me. They were so good to me. My mum was desperate to give them some money, not that we could afford much, but of course James's mum wouldn't hear a word of it. And James's dad is someone who I really look up to as a really strong-minded, cool person who I could talk to about anything. Having said this, I think to be honest that James and I were pissed almost all the time – we'd be getting into all the local student union bars and taking advantage of their cheap beer.

We were really living the student life, except

without the work.

Actually, that's probably just what the student life is like. The funny thing is that while me and James were scumming it up in dodgy student clubs, Charlie was still at boarding school having these ridiculous balls, where they'd have waiters and proper dinners, hanging out with millionaire rich kids and Winston Churchill's great-grandson!

James: I loved having Mattie staying round my house – it was like having another brother in the family, though I don't think any of my brothers were ever quite as messy as Mattie became. One night out from that period really sticks in my mind. Neither of us were very experienced on the London club scene but we decided that we wanted to go to this place called Sugar Reef, which is supposed to be really exclusive but we've since discovered is full of Page Three models and EastEnders actors.

Mattie: We got to the club and of course we hadn't been invited and had no reason to be there so we spent about twenty minutes at the door giving the bouncer hassle, trying to persuade him to let us in. I was going, 'Yeah, man, we're a band, we're in the top ten.' This was at a time when we'd barely written a single song! We weren't very convincing and were told in no uncertain terms to sling our hook. Ever since we've actually been in the top ten, we haven't been back at all and the irony is that while we could probably get into most 'exclusive' clubs these days, we've noticed that most clubs in London are rubbish. They tend to be full of people looking out for famous people, just for the sake of seeing who's there. We'd much rather just go down the local pub for a pint and some crisps.

James: When we were about to sign to Universal Island, we decided that Southend was probably not the most practical of locations, so finding a flat in

London seemed a sensible idea. We looked at loads of places – and met some right dodgy landlords in the process – but eventually found somewhere in north London which was perfect.

(My definition of 'perfect' is 'Lots of light when the sun's out, and enough room for a ping-pong table.')

The thing is, I wasn't actually with Charlie and Mattie when they found the house, and they were pretty crafty about the whole thing. They came back talking about their rooms, which I found a bit suspicious. They were going on about, 'Oh yeah, James, your room is in the middle – it's a really interesting shape.' The phrase 'interesting shape' rang some alarm bells. I went round and saw it and, as I had suspected,

'interesting shape' obviously meant the same as when estate agents say 'Ideal for a DIY enthusiast'. It was ridiculous! So I insisted that we drew straws and as it happened I ended up with a great room with en-suite bathroom, and Charlie had the crap room!

Mattie: We moved in towards the end of February 2002. The flat is in a big block which sounds like some sort of pop theme park – Girls Aloud, Damage and Sean from Five live there, and I think someone from Blue is considering moving in soon too. I was most excited about the fact that the boxer Lennox Lewis had a penthouse flat there, until I discovered that it was actually a flat he'd bought for his mum. I still have plans to befriend him through his mother, though – I'm determined to carry her shopping for her one day, and worm my way in that way! Personally, I loved the flat when we moved in and I still love it now. It's loads bigger than the house I grew up in, for a start,

though I would say the area's a bit poncey for my liking. A lot of the people think that we're too young to live in a nice flat and that we haven't earned our place there yet.

There are a lot of rich bankers there,

and if you're familiar with Cockney rhyming slang you'll probably know what I'm getting at. But our money's as good as anybody else's – and some people just have a problem with teenagers!

James: As soon as we moved in, we drove down to the Ikea furniture warehouse in Croydon, really excited about buying stuff for the home. Next door have got a really good balcony garden so we were going to try and out-do them – we picked up palm trees for the balcony, tables, rugs, piled up our shopping trolleys and... Mattie's card was declined at the checkout! We had

two massive trolleys full of stuff and no way of paying for it, so we said we'd go and get some cash and legged it. We've never dared go back since – maybe all the stuff is still there now.

Mattie: We were a bit noisy for the first few weeks in that house. One time there was all this banging on the wall and when I went to see what was going on there was some guy – four foot tall with pink slippers and a stupid dog, a bit like the male Geri Halliwell – giving me a right earful. So obviously I told him where to go and slammed the door. When I turned round, James and Charlie emerged from a room where they'd been hiding, and explained that they'd been playing the drums with the door wide open! And I was the one who got the bollocking for it! Then there was another time I was having a party with some mates: music on, bit of ping-pong, that kind of thing. Suddenly all the electricity went off!

The guy in the pink slippers had only gone and turned our power off!

But that's given us a good idea for whenever people piss us off in the flat: we'll just cut their power. But even though we've had a few problems, having a flat in London is amazing. I was the first of my mates to move out of home, and I was really proud of my new place. It also gave each of us an opportunity to meet each other's friends. Charlie didn't know what to expect of my mates – to be honest, I was probably the first working-class person he'd ever met in his life and he thought all my mates were going to be little Trevors. But he ended up getting on so well with them – he went, 'Mattie, I'm really impressed, they're all really well-dressed', as if he expected them to be wearing sack-cloth like Victorian urchins or something!
Charlie: Some people are quite surprised at how tidy the flat is. It's never

pristine, but

we all like to keep the place looking spick and span.

My room's quite minimal – a lava lamp my parents bought me, some Bart Simpson stuff, a drumkit and guitar, my clothes, and that's about it. James is probably the tidiest of us all and Mattie has little piles of clutter in his room but he insists that he knows where everything is. I certainly know where his stereo is, because I was bored when I was cooking one afternoon and decided to unplug it from his bedroom and move it into the kitchen.

James: If there's one under-used part of the flat, it's probably the kitchen. None of us are big on cooking, although Mattie has just figured out how to do a wicked pasta carbonara which he cooks every week now, and I've discovered a bit of a

talent for making pancakes. Mattie says that's because I'm a champion tosser, which is a bit harsh! The dishwasher rarely gets emptied, either. Sometimes half of it's full of clean plates and the other half is full of dirty plates, but we're all a bit too busy, and a bit too lazy, to spend twenty minutes putting things back in cupboards.

Charlie: I loved living with Mattie and James but in February 2003, I moved out of the Busted house. My new flat's not quite as big as the Busted flat, but I'm enjoying a bit of independence, and it means that I have a bit of time and space to reflect on my own life. It's probably a hangover from my old boarding school days – the idea of being with people 24/7 still worries me a little. So far the new arrangement has worked out fine – though I think the guys are a little annoyed that these days I can't always give them a lift home every time we go out!

Girls

MATT

For a long time I thought romance was a bit overrated and a bit sappy, and it wasn't until I met someone who meant a lot to me that I realised I wanted a way of expressing how I felt. Valentine's Day may be a bit of a con as far as I'm concerned, but there are plenty of other ways to be romantic, and they don't all have to be clichéd.

My romantic career began when I was about nine years old. My family owned a caravan down on Sussex Beach, on the south coast, and sometimes they'd let me take my friends down there too. One time, this girl had snogged two of my friends, who were one year older than me, but she wouldn't kiss me because I was too young. Then one day the other two took the mickey out of her – I think they called her a rubbish kisser – and she ran off crying. I was despatched to tell her not to cry, and I did the whole shoulder-to-cry-on business, and we ended up snogging! I

knew I was going to do it, she knew I was going to do it. Mission accomplished. (My friends were right, though: she was a bit of a rubbish kisser.)

After that, I never looked back.

I had loads of girlfriends when I was at school

my first was a year younger than me, but quite fit, so that was okay. The problem with really fit birds, as any bloke knows, is that they tend to end up cheating on you, as this girl did. She was at a party and got off with some other bloke, so I dumped her after three triumphant weeks. The worst-ever date was when I took a girl out for dinner. At one point she was sipping some wine, then spontaneously spluttered and coughed it everywhere. Then she carried on eating her dinner, with half-drunk wine all over it! That didn't go well. I was always a bit hit-and-miss with girls. I never had girlfriends for very

long, and even my first proper girlfriend when I was sixteen didn't last longer than a year. When we started going out, she'd actually just split up with one of my best friends, so perhaps it was doomed to failure, but that relationship did mean a lot to me. As for the future – well, I like strong, feminine women. And I like girls who are intelligent, with their head screwed on, who can tell me when I'm letting myself down but do so without nagging me. I'd like to think I'm a good boyfriend but I'm not always as thoughtful as I could be, especially since I'm also an outrageous flirt which always gets me into trouble, even though I don't really mean it. I don't know all the nice restaurants, or how to behave on a date, but I do things in my own way. And that seems to work just fine.

JAMES

Is there such a thing as an original romantic? If there is, then that's how I'd classify myself – I like going in for romance, but I'd never do the whole 'candlelit baths and red roses' routine.

I'd classify myself as an original romantic.

Of course, girls love it when you do give them flowers, but I find that they like it even more when you do something totally out of the ordinary. I think the secret is to surprise people – like if you're not expecting to see someone and they sprint round your house late at night just to say hello. Short-notice holidays are great too, if you grab her passport and go, 'Pack your bags – we're getting on a plane and we're going to Hawaii.'

Since I was quite young, my romantic history has seen a few missed opportunities and wasted moments, so I've learned now that when something comes along you have to grab it, or her, with both hands. The first girl I ever liked, for example, is someone I had a huge crush on – but never told her even though I was obsessed with her for about two years! She still doesn't know...

Just as I was about to do something about the mystery girl, I decided that someone else rocked my world even more than she did, who was a girl called Kara. When I first asked her on a date, she totally blew me out, but after a week she changed her mind and went on to be the most long-term girlfriend I've ever had. We were together until I was sixteen, but it's one of those relationships that just ended really horribly. At that point I'd just dropped out of my course at college and her career – she's an actress now – was really picking up. I don't think I was a very good prospect as a boyfriend, really. And that was that – I left to go to London.

I dated a girl called Amandine for a short while after that, which lasted for a few weeks before I realised I was still into Kara. The night I split up with Amandine

was a disaster – I went round to her house having been out with Matt, so I was slightly drunk. I told her it wasn't really working out and she actually didn't seem particularly upset, then I discovered that

I'd managed to lock myself out of my house

and had to break in through a really small, really high kitchen window.

I woke up the next morning and, as a sign of how drunk I'd actually been, I realised that I'd put bananas everywhere. I was hung-over and covered in scrapes and grazes from climbing in through the window. More to the point, I had no girlfriend. If life is a series of peaks and valleys, at that point I felt like I was at being swept along by the river right at the bottom of the valley. Later that day I realised that, in love as in the rest of life, you can't dwell on problems because they'll only get worse:

Since then my approach to both areas of life has been a lot brighter…

CHARLIE

I've definitely been approached by more girls since I joined the band, which I think must be some sort of cosmic payback for all those years I was cooped up at boarding school with nothing but boys as far as the eye could see! In fact

I was fourteen by the time I had my first girlfriend.

She was a couple of years older than me, as all the girls at Uppingham were, because girls were only allowed in the sixth form, and I think that's probably how I developed my thing for older women.

As well as being my first girlfriend, she was also the first girl that I got really intimate with, but unfortunately, as it

later turned out, she was a psycho. I'm prepared to admit that I was partly at fault for the way we split up (basically I went off with one of her best friends at a party), but the way she reacted was so over-the-top that I realised I was better off without her! I think the crunch point came when her brother phoning me at odd hours threatening to kill me. That girl has since turned up in a couple of songs – one called 'One Sixteen' which is quite a suicidal song, but only in the sense that suicide would have been the only way to get away from her. And I wrote another song about her recently, 'The Peaceful Way Of Letting Go'. But that's also about suicide.

While some girls are capable only of bringing out my gloomy side, I met one girl at Uppingham who changed all of that. Her name's Camilla. Camilla was two years older than me, and she was the biggest part of my life, apart from my music, for such a long time. My friends would get annoyed that I spent too much

time with her, but she was too important to me. Pretty much all the songs I've written over the past few years have been about her – 'Without You' is one of them, which seems incredibly poignant now, as Camilla and I split up early on in 2003. With all the time I was spending on Busted, it had become really difficult making time for her, and I felt that I was being really unfair. It was an awful decision to have to make, because Camilla is the first girl I've ever been in love with, but we're still really good friends so maybe, one day in the future, we can sort something out.

In the meantime, I'm single.

I like to think I'm quite a romantic guy

one Valentine's Day I did the whole thing with rose petals round the bath, candles and champagne, which went down quite well, and I love the idea of walking down deserted beaches with a girl. I like girls to be quick-witted and bright, preferably blonde (though I'm open to persuasion) and quite independent. For example, I don't mind being chatted up by a girl, and one thing I certainly didn't mind at all was when I was at a party recently and Dannii Minogue went 'Fwooorggh!' as I walked past, which is one of the most proud achievements of my entire life. Nothing happened, though. Well, not yet, anyway...

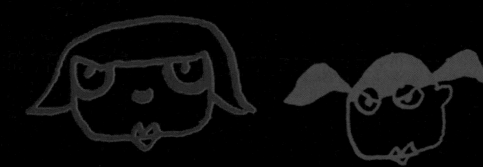

On The Road

James: I love being on stage more than anything else in the world. You can get away with doing whatever the hell you want and there are no rules, so when we first found out that we'd be touring in May 2003 it was a really important moment for the band. We love being in the studio, making videos and appearing on the TV, but

nothing beats actually being on stage

and performing like you do on tour. The travelling is always a real laugh, even though Charlie's not too fond of flying, so I always make sure I sit next to him and pull frightened faces when we're taking off, just to freak him out a little bit more.

Mattie: The thing with big gigs is that too often people at the back will miss out on stuff, I really strive to make people at the back feel as if they're right in the mosh-pit. Dave Grohl from the Foo

Fighters sets a really good example as far as this is concerned – when I saw him last it was at Wembley Arena. Obviously that's a huge venue, but he genuinely made every single person in the room feel wanted. Cheesy audience participation isn't something I go in for, but I'd hate for someone to walk away from our concert thinking it was boring –

I want everyone to come out having had a great time.

And I think they did!

Charlie: Playing live is why I got into music, and being on stage is a feeling you just can't beat. One really memorable gig that we played early on was at G-A-Y in London, which was amazing but so weird. Up until that point we'd been playing shows for teenage girls, who were screaming and grabbing

us and stuff, and we went to G-A-Y and the guys were doing exactly the same thing! Apparently Mattie is their favourite – but that night was a bit of a weird one for Mattie because the whole thing was themed around a school disco. Korben from Pop Idol was performing, and he was head boy, while Sonia was head girl.

Somehow we ended up being milk monitors.

Milk monitors! Mattie's brother's band was playing a gig round the corner on the same night and when they drove past G-A-Y they saw the hoarding with us as milk monitors and phoned him up to take the piss. Matt found that all a bit baffling.

James: One of the things with touring is that there tends to be loads of downtime, and when we don't have something to do we usually start getting into trouble. Matt's the worst – he always ends up

64

getting into really odd sorts of mischief. Usually it's stuff like throwing fruit out of windows to passengers in open-topped buses, but there was one time when we were in Germany and I walked past Matt's room, which was on the fifth floor, to see him hanging out of the window.

I walked past Matt's room to see him hanging out of the window.

He wasn't standing on anything, he was just hanging there. I asked him if he was all right, and he went, 'I'm fine, just a bit bored.' Matt had actually climbed out onto the window ledge because he was so bored. We made sure he had access to a DVD player after that, as we don't have any intention of going down to a duo quite yet!

Mattie: I've also got into reading in a big way. I'm reading Michael J Fox's memoirs at the moment, and have just finished a book called The Dice Man, which is about a guy who lives his life according to what's on a dice and ends up doing some seriously weird stuff as a result. I still get distracted by hotels, though, and

I've got the worst room service bill of them all.

It's a disgrace. The thing is, to start with I had to pay my own phone bills from hotel rooms — which are really expensive because hotels always set them at a premium rate. And then, sometime early in 2003, I stopped being billed for my phone calls. Nobody explained why, but it was like a red rag to a bull and ever since I've been totally hammering the phones in all the hotels we stay in. We've actually managed to get ourselves banned from one chain of hotels. We accidentally got really, really pissed one night and ran riot throughout the entire place, and as a consequence we're not allowed to stay there again.

The funny thing is that every other act on our record label, Universal Island, is banned too, so we're quite pleased with ourselves on that front.

Charlie: We're pretty oddly behaved in hotels, but not always in a bad way. There was one time when we were on tour — we'd had a bit to drink after the show, and we were on our way back. It was a bitterly cold night and certainly not the kind of night you'd want to be outside at all. We passed this homeless guy, who probably wasn't that much older than any of us.

After we'd given him all our loose change, we decided to invite him back to the hotel. We walked him into our hotel, then up in the lifts and up to our room. And I think up until the point where we actually arrived in our room, the guy thought we'd been taking the mick or something, but we got there, let him have a bath, ordered him some room service and left him to it. Not

65

something we told our management about because we probably would have got told off, but it was nice to help the guy out.

James: Another good thing about going out on tour is that you get to meet up with friends who are also in bands. Lee from Blue is one person it's always fun to meet up with – and believe me when I say that he's more rock and roll than a lot of rock stars we meet! One time we met up with him in Munich and got so hammered on B52s, White Russian cocktails, tequilas, beers ... We've got video footage of one point in the evening and we just look as if we're about to die. At one point Lee disappeared with some fans then when we got back to the hotel we found out that we were locked out. Matt and Charlie decided to go to sleep on the pavement outside the hotel but eventually we were let in by a night porter who bore a terrifying resemblance to Lurch from The Addams Family. So I went to bed and, predictably, the next

morning we were running late for the flight home. I got a key for Matt and Charlie's room, walked in and there was vomit. Everywhere. Charlie had been sick all over the bedroom floor, then crawled to the end of his bed, opened Matt's bag and been sick in that too!

The journey to the airport after that was a total trauma. The cab driver got pulled over for speeding, and Mattie was on the back seat yelling, 'IT'S ALL MY FAULT! IT'S ALL MY FAULT!' without any shoes or socks on because he'd somehow lost them the previous night. We got to the airport and I had to go and buy Matt some shoes from Duty Free, but nobody was talking to him because we'd decided it was his fault we'd all got drunk. We missed our flight and had to get new tickets, and all the way home in that airplane cabin, all we could smell was last night's vomit. The Head of International at the record label gave us a serious bollocking over that – and the fact that

they'd had to pay an extra £8,000 for later flights.

Not one of our better nights on the town, as it turned out.

Mattie: Being on tour means that we get the opportunity to meet our fans, and they're really different all around the world. In Germany, for example, they can be quite extreme, and all the stuff they get up to really makes us laugh. For example German fans will follow us down the motorway for a hundred miles with their lights off, thinking we can't see them, as if it's inconspicuous for a car to be driving at night without its lights on. Then they'll book into the hotel we're staying at! And the Mexican girls you just would not believe – they must be the hottest country on earth. The strange thing is that when you're living in hotels so much that the only people you tend to meet are other

tourists, so we'll be in Italy but end up spending your time with more Americans, German and French people than you will actual Italians. You can't beat British fans, though. A couple of weeks ago I went back to my mum's house and someone had posted through the door a painting of the band. It was just amazing. There was no name on it, no address, no nothing. They didn't want anything back for it and they didn't even want recognition for it. They just painted us. I've sent the painting off to be framed – it's something I really want to keep. One thing I would say, is that some of the banners the fans make are absolutely filthy.

The things they say even make me blush, and that takes some doing. And as for the amount of girls who whip their tops off when we're on stage ... Well, it can sometimes be a bit of a distraction! James: The first time we ever realised we had fans was a very, very weird moment. We were at a Party In The Park

in 2002 and we just got accosted by loads of girls. Charlie was being hilarious, because he decided that he 'didn't belong' there because of his indie ethic. In all the early pictures of Charlie with fans he's got an utter face like thunder. Our first ever fans were two girls called Gem and Rachel – I remember standing with them watching Blue performing on stage. They were, like, 'Well, this time next year you'll be on stage.' They're really nice people. They're fun to talk to – we talk to them like mates now.

Mattie: It's really nice knowing that you can trust your fans. A lot of them know where we live but they always respect our private time. And they're so dedicated. If we're at a studio we'll hang around for a bit and chat to them outside, then jump in our car and go to the next studio. And by the time we arrive at the next place – the fans are already there! Joining fans who'd been waiting there. So then they'll all follow

us to the next place. And the group just keeps getting bigger.

James: I love to travel so obviously

being in Busted is a dream job.

We went to Sweden at the start of 2003 and discovered that, over the road from the restaurant we were in, was a club that was owned by Max Martin – my absolute songwriting hero. As soon as I found out I got up from the table and ran over the road to see if he was there, but I was told that he'd left, literally five minutes earlier! I'd hate him to think of me as a stalker, but at the same time one day I will meet him.

Sweden was fine, but sometimes it can be difficult finding common ground with international work colleagues. I remember we did an international conference with our Japanese label at one point and the only thing I had in

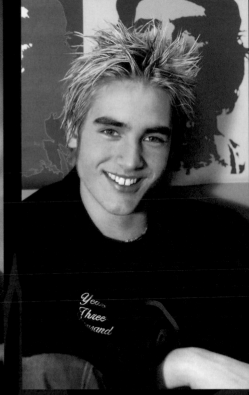

Busted around the world...

Mishal Varma,
Vice President of Network
Programming, MTV Asia

'We've been getting a lot of requests from Taiwan and the South East Asian markets and, being in Singapore, I can tell you that radio over here has gone really big on "Year 3000". English is not a familiar language here but Busted have done really well because of having a really good attitude to working over here – I think, like everywhere else in the world, Busted's music has done so well because it's so different from everything else that has been offered. We're expecting them to be a really big act over here for the next few years.'

common with the guy I was talking to was the Backstreet Boys – so we ended up talked about the ins and outs of Black & Blue for half an hour, rather than anything to do with Busted!

My big ambition for the band is to make an impression in America. It's notoriously difficult to get heard out there, but I love that country almost as much as I like Britain and one of my dreams is to play on TRL with Carson Daly. But I guess we'll cross that bridge when we get to it...

Time Out

CHARLIE

Life in Busted did go through a phase where we had no time off whatsoever, but these days we do have scheduled days off, which has been an utter godsend. Even so, time off is so rare that, when it does come, I've really learned to cherish every moment of it. Something I always try to make time for is the chance to see my family.

While I'm home I'll either go and see my friends or jam with musicians I know outside of Busted. Sometimes I'll even record some music with them; in fact I'm planning soon to lay down some tracks with some friends from my childhood bands, which will be real fun. I doubt we'll end up releasing any of it, but it should make an interesting experiment.

Another passion of mine is going to the cinema. My friends all take the piss out of the fact that I've got such a movie-going ritual – they say I behave like I'm middle-aged – but everything has to be just right. For a start, I need to get there in time to buy sweets and popcorn, which has to be salty, because

sweet popcorn is putrid.

Then I find my seat, which always has to be right in the middle of the audience. And I need to get there in time for the trailers, too. (I don't think I'm the most relaxing of people to go to the movies with, to be honest.)

I could talk about movies all day – after music, they're the thing I'm most passionate about. I love films that get my mind working, and I'll often come out of the cinema continuing the story in my head, wondering what happens next. I love the film Memento, starring Guy Pearce, which is told backwards. Then there are films like American History X and The Basketball Diaries, films about what it's like to be young with really serious issues to try and resolve. Sometime in the future I'd actually love

a small part in an indie film – something like Clerks or Mallrats. It'd have to be an American film, though, because I tend to find that British ones are usually full of unconvincing gangster types talking about birds and guns, which gets rather boring when you see it for the umpteenth time.

Going back to Woodbridge is a brilliant chance to escape from the non-stop mania of living in London – it's a really quiet place. Not the kind of place you'd go if you wanted a 'cool' time – but the walks are amazing. There's a river running through Woodbridge and a boatyard just down the road from my house, where I'll often go and catch up on my thoughts. It's so peaceful there, and a million miles away from life on the road with Mattie and James!

JAMES

It's sometimes really easy to get swept along in the Busted bubble and, though I hate to admit it, sometimes it's even

easy to forget that you have a life outside the band. For this reason I make a real effort to get out of London, and back to Southend, as much as I can, because my mates back at home never treat me any differently from when I was still struggling away on my music course at college. I guess it's like Busted's another coursework assignment, in a way.

People think that if they break into the music industry and are rarely home they lose their roots, but no matter how long it is between visits I still feel that I can go back, go to a bar, play a bit of pool and have a laugh with my mates. All my good friends know me really well, and they know it's been my aim to get into music all my life, so I think they're all really pleased for me. It's good when you can have a group of friends who won't be any different towards you.

One place I really like to go on my days off is a beach hut down in Southend. My mum and dad bought it with my best friend Tom's mum and dad, and we've had it since I was really small. It was always a refuge for me and Tom when we were younger – it's a lovely, peaceful beach and in the summer it was amazing to go down there and just knock around with my mates. When I'm back home I'll meet up with Tom and we'll often go down there together, and it's literally as if we're ten again.

Catching up with my family is really important, too.

Now I know what older relatives always meant when they said I was growing up quickly – my little brother Chris is ten now, and even if it's just a month since I last saw him, he's always changed so much.

Then there's the tennis club I always used to practise at – the Thorpe Bay Lawn Tennis Club. I remember that when I was a member and I used to play social at the end of the evening, it was always difficult to find someone to have a knockabout with. These days I'll go down and people will be fighting over who gets to lose to me!

MATTIE
It's rare for us to get time to ourselves, so when we do it's something we really try to make the most of, and our management have become quite good at wangling us days off here and there. It's great that Molesey is quite close to London, because it means that I can get down there in the evening and go to see my mates. I love the band but sometimes it's nice to forget all about Busted – and being with my mates, it's almost as if I've never left Molesey. In a way

I live a totally different life from most of my mates,

but I don't think any of them consider me to be any different from a couple of years ago, and they certainly don't treat me any differently at all, which is a nice relief from people in the music business sucking up to me all the time. For example they'll always be the first to take the piss out of a shirt I was wearing on CD:UK. It's great to just be one of the boys again, and in a way to take off the Busted persona, and catch up on who's been getting off with who, or whatever, without having the fact that I've got to go to Germany in the back of my mind.

Going back to see my mates helps me to keep Mattie the pop star separate from Mattie the bloke from Molesey, which is really important for me as it's really easy in this business to get caught up in a lifestyle and, before you know it, you've totally lost the plot! I love going to gigs too. It used to be a real mission – I had no transport or money or anything, and we'd always have to leave before the end to get the last train home. £14 for a

ticket? I had to buy beer with that money! But in London everything's on my doorstep, and I've got a bit of cash to be able to buy tickets.

Something I haven't done for ages is go fishing, which I really want to get back into. My dad's a really keen fisherman and I used to love it. My mum used to tell me off for going out and fishing at night (and I'd always get caught because obviously I'd arrive home stinking of fish), but it was so relaxing. Well, apart from the occasion when I swallowed a maggot after my mate threw a load at me and one went in my mouth. People call fishing really boring, but it's not. You've got your fishing rod, your cans of beer, your stereo (kept really quiet so you don't scare the fish), your mates … It's not really about catching fish at all – it's about getting away from it all. And sometimes that's just what you need.

Looking To The Future

CHARLIE

I've given up on trying to find a non-corny way of saying this, but the success I've had with Busted really has been like a dream come true.

As far as the future goes, there's a second album to record, and I can't wait to get into the studio – which apart from being on stage is my favourite place on earth, though hopefully this time round we won't have to dodge quite as many leaky ceilings! I love Busted, but something I'd like to push towards a bit with the second one is to get real drums in there, and to make it a bit more authentic. We've had some really exciting talks with producers we really admire, and whose work has been stuff we've all listened to in the past, so hopefully the second album will be even better – and, if I've got anything to do with it,

the second album will sound a lot more 'live'

74

than the first,

mainly because I hope to be drumming on the tracks. A load of great songs have come out of our writing sessions and I know there's a lot pressure on the second album, but as far as I'm concerned, the main pressure will be to make another album I love.

Ultimately, when I'm a lot older, I may even put together my own supergroup – there are dozens of talented musicians I'd love to work with, and who'd be able to teach me loads about songwriting. (I've always wanted to create some sort of orchestra of rock with dozens of guitarists, and me conducting them, though everyone keeps tell me that's a stupid idea and I think, ultimately, that they might be right. Time will tell!) In my personal life, I want to make sure that I'm always happy doing what I'm doing. That's important to me. Anything I do needs to make me happy. I don't want to end up doing something I don't

want to do, and that's something I'm quite apprehensive about. I also really want to settle down with the right girl, and have a couple of kids. I still really miss my last proper girlfriend, Camilla, who I mentioned earlier on in the book. So hopefully at some time in the future I'll find someone who means as much to me as she did.

MATT

I've never before in my life been focused on anything, but

music's the first thing that's really obsessed me.

Even so, I've got a lot of things to do in my life, things that I have to do. I want to be able to look back in ten years, having released eight albums, and go, 'Look at that. Look what I've done.' And I'd like those albums to show me as someone who you can never overestimate. But

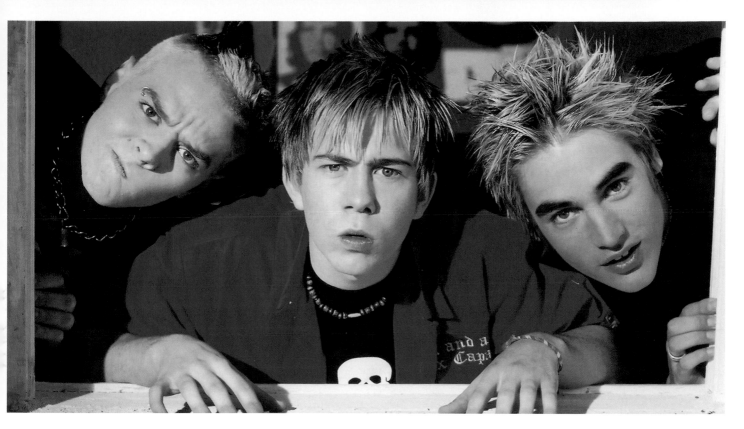

more than that, I want to know that my family are proud of me, and I always want to do good by them. Going off and being in a band isn't the sort of thing that's ever been done before in my family: people would sometimes go off to college or something, but they'd usually drop out. I'd like to be a success.

Buying my mum a car is something I really cherish having done, and it'd be great to be able to buy her a home in a slightly nicer area, because she's still living in quite a rough part of town. Getting somewhere of my own is quite important too – but I don't intend to settle down for a while, and you won't find me with a golfing umbrella down the park walking my dogs anytime soon. Although, thinking about it, a couple of dogs would be cool. Just without the golfing umbrella.

For Busted, the second album will be something that really tests us, as songwriters and as a band, and I can't wait to really get my teeth into it. A lot of bands fall into a false sense of security, and sometimes arrogance, when they come to their second album, but I love all the 'Year 3000's and 'What I Go To School For's on the first album and I think it would be a real shame to lose the humour in the future, so that's something we're definitely going to try and keep in while, at the same time, not falling into the trap of being a gimmick band like a lot of groups do.

I love writing fun songs and hearing fun songs,

so Busted will still be Busted. I'll always enjoy writing radio-friendly songs, but one subject I really want to write about is the feeling when you first realise you're falling in love. It's something I never thought I'd experience, and then one day I did. So that'll make a great song sometime in the future.
I love Busted. I think we're a good little group. And we're still kicking the crap

out of pop music. Hopefully we'll continue to do that for years to come.

JAMES
I've learned more in the past eighteen months than I learned in the rest of my life put together, and I feel like

I've done more with Busted than I'd ever done before.

I feel that Busted has educated me in essential ways that I would never have known from school, and one of the most important lessons I've learned has been about people skills – getting on with people, making the most of your time with people, just generally being a rounded human being. It's one of the most important things in life, and it's amazing that Busted has given me the chance to learn that. But I know that I've still got loads to learn, and in ten years time I hope I'll know everything about

myself, and the people I love. That's precisely where I'd like to find myself.

In the long term, I know that a band like Busted isn't going to last forever, but I know that music can take you down a lot of different avenues. And it doesn't always have to mean being in a pop group. I've already mentioned Max Martin in this book, and I think his career path is really interesting – he started off in a band, then in his twenties he moved into songwriting and production and went on to write some of the greatest pop music I've ever heard. And then, after he'd conquered the world with songs for people like Britney and 'NSYNC, he decided to go right back to the beginning. He had enough money not to need to make any more, so he began choosing smaller artists who wouldn't have been able to afford his services, and he worked with them for next to nothing. Every part of that career appeals to me, and in years to come I'd like to be able to help people out and

give them the opportunity in the same way I was nurtured by people like my own management.

Something else I'd really like to explore is the idea of working as a film composer. John Williams, who wrote the scores to films like ET, Jaws and Star Wars, is another of my musical heroes, and I love the idea of music bringing an idea to life, a bit like Busted have done with the things we write about. So perhaps a bit of soundtrack work would be great to get involved with in a few years. And aside from James from Busted, there's James Bourne the person. I'm not sure exactly when I'm going to start a family – finding the right girl would be a good start, obviously, and there's loads I want to do before I settle down – but I really want kids and I want to be a young father, so that's something to start thinking about sooner rather than later. Oh, and I want a chimp. But that's for another book…

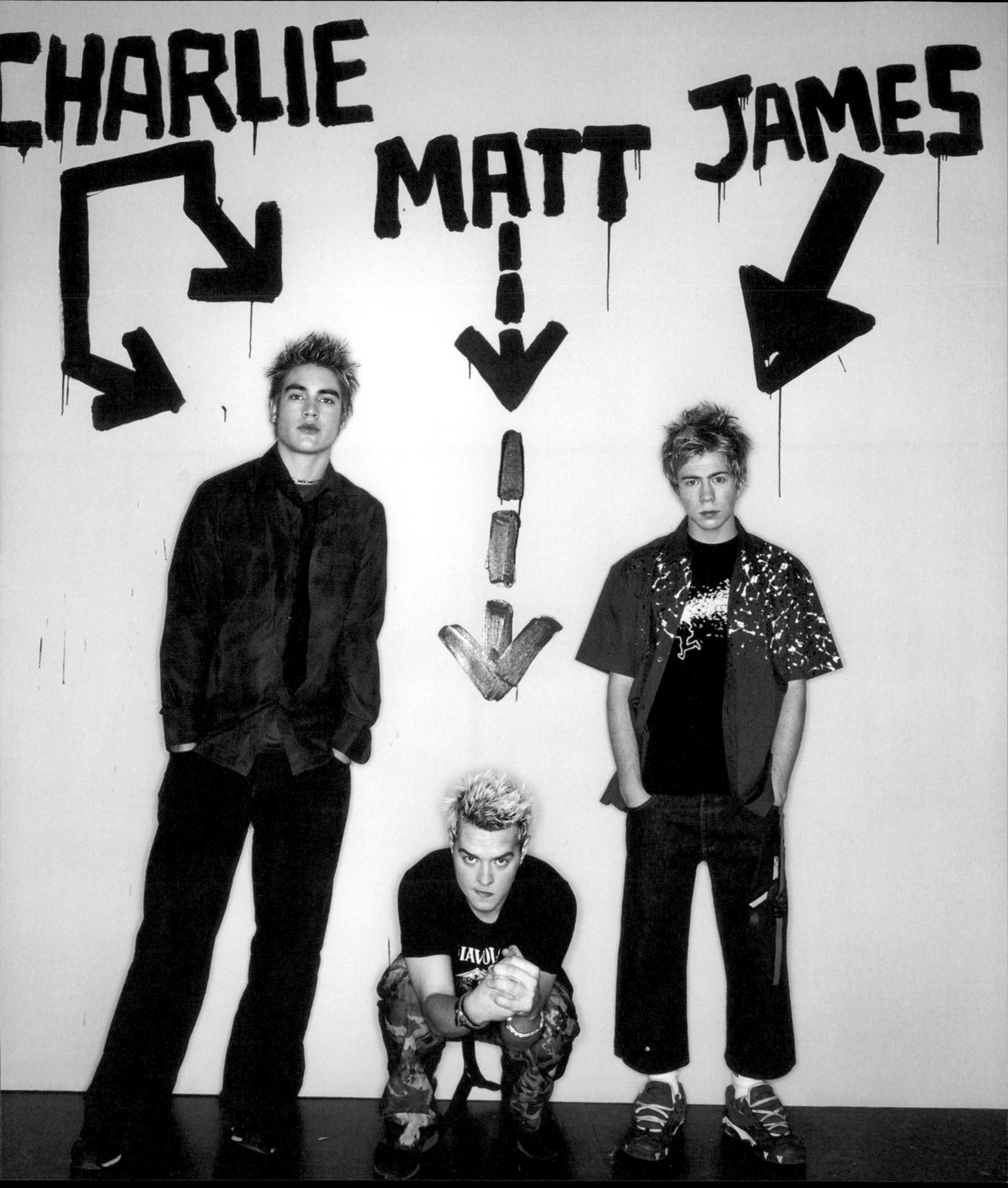
CHARLIE
MATT
JAMES

Busted would like to thank: Mr Gammon, Donald Mcinnes, Charlotte Cave, Form, Ellis Parrinder, James McMillan, D·Fi, Kiehl's and MAC

The awesome debut album from Busted is out now. 13 tracks including the Top 3 singles 'What I Go To School For' and 'Year 3000' plus the massive Number 1, 'You Said No'. Special edition enhanced album includes loads of interactive extras.

 www..com